U.S. Decennial Life Tables for 1989-91

I0415774

Volume II, State Life Tables Number 3, Arizona

From the CENTERS FOR DISEASE CONTROL AND PREVENTION/National Center for Health Statistics

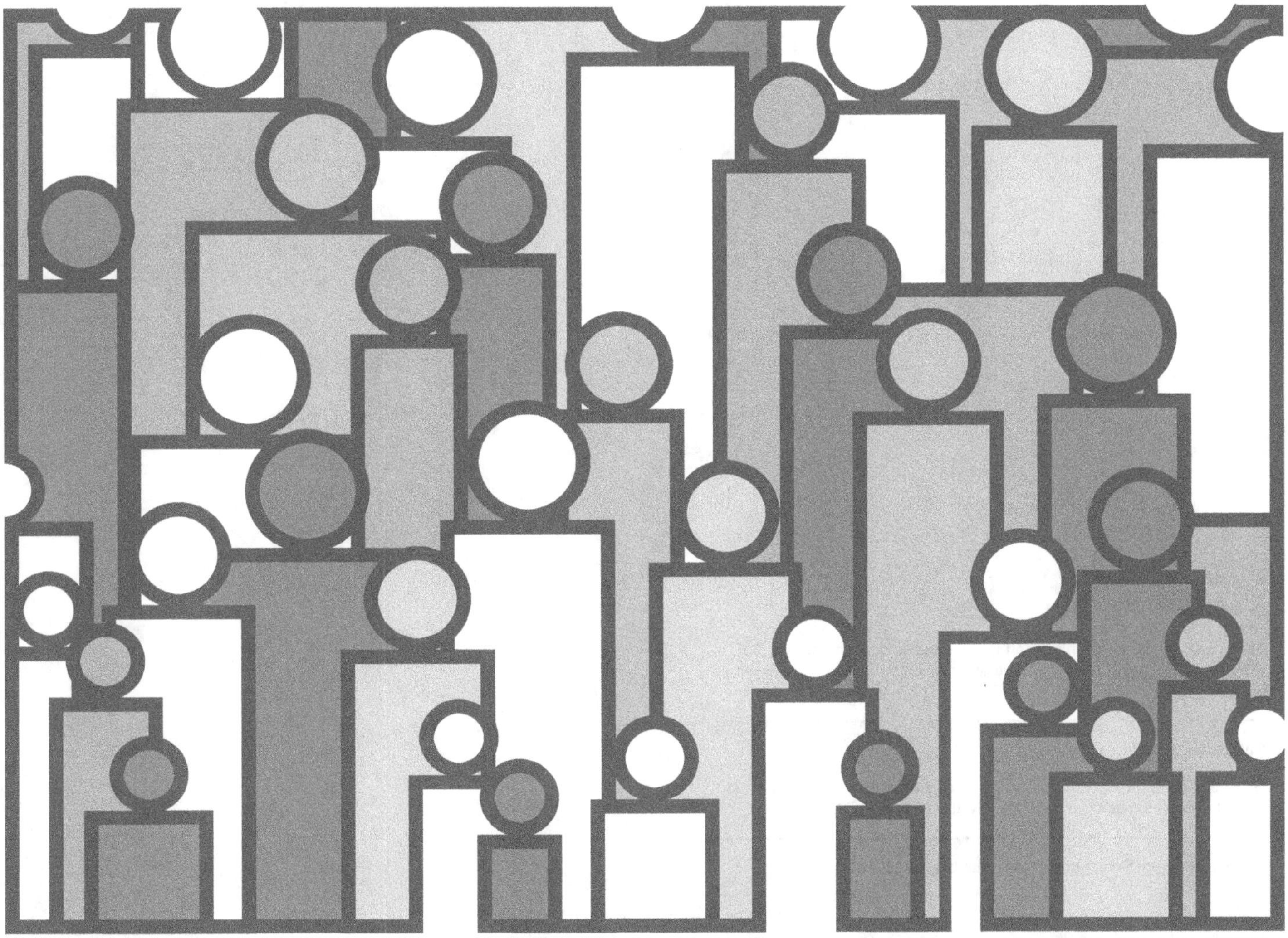

U.S. DEPARTMENT OF HEALTH AND HUMAN SERVICES
Centers for Disease Control and Prevention
National Center for Health Statistics

Suggested citation

Na ional Center for Health Statistics. U.S. decennial life tables for 1989–91, vol II, State life tables no. 3, Arizona. Hyattsville, Maryland. 1998.

Library of Congress Catalog Card Number 85-600190

For sale by the U.S. Government Printing Office
Superintendent of Documents
Mail Stop: SSOP
Washington, DC 20402-9328

U.S. Decennial
Life Tables
for 1989-91

Volume II, State Life Tables Number 3, Arizona

U.S. DEPARTMENT OF HEALTH AND HUMAN SERVICES
Centers for Disease Control and Prevention
National Center for Health Statistics

Hyattsville, Maryland
March 1998

DHHS Publication No. PHS-98-1151-3

Contents

Acknowledgments

This report was prepared in the Division of Vital Statistics (DVS) under the guidance of an ad hoc committee chaired by Robert J. Armstrong and included Stephen C. Goss and Alice H. Wade of the Office of the Actuary, Social Security Administration; Gregory K. Spencer and Frederick W. Hollmann of the U.S. Bureau of the Census; and David P. Johnson, Lester R. Curtin, Nonie Atkinson, Kenneth D. Kochanek, Harry M. Rosenberg, Jeffrey D. Maurer, and Joseph D. Farrell from the National Center for Health Statistics.

Nonie Atkinson, formerly of the Office of Research and Methodology (ORM), was responsible for the overall computer systems analysis and design, and played a major role in writing the programs to produce the life tables and their variances. Lester R. Curtin, also of ORM, consulted on methodological issues including the preparation of standard errors for the life tables.

Joseph D. Farrell, Charles E. Royer, and David P. Johnson of the Systems, Programming, and Statistical Resources Branch, DVS, coordinated data processing and developed computer processes that eased the workload of the actuarial statistician and the Publications Branch. They also provided major programming support in summarizing data basic to the calculation of the life tables.

Gregory K. Spencer and Frederick W. Hollmann of the U.S. Bureau of the Census furnished the modified-race populations that were used in the production of these tables.

Stephen C. Goss, Felicite C. Bell, and Bertram M. Kestenbaum of the Office of the Actuary, Social Security Administration, provided mortality data from the Medicare program that were used at age 85 years and over. Vanetta A. Harrington of the Systems, Programming, and Statistical Resources Branch, DVS, provided content review, and Robert N. Anderson of the Mortality Statistics Branch, DVS, provided peer review. This report was edited by Gail Johnson and typeset by Zung T. N. Le of the Publications Branch, Division of Data Services.

Arizona Life Tables: 1989–91

by Robert J. Armstrong, M.S.,
Division of Vital Statistics

Abstract

The life tables in this report are current life tables for Arizona based on age-specific death rates for the period 1989–91. The death rates were calculated using data from the 1990 census of population and deaths occurring in the United States to residents of Arizona in the 3 years 1989–91. Presented are tables for the white population, the population other than white, and the black population, separately by sex and for both sexes combined, and also for the total population and for total males and total females. Standard errors of the probability of dying and of life expectancy are also provided.

Introduction

The life tables in this report are current life tables for Arizona based on age-specific death rates for the period 1989–91. With the exception of those for ages 95 years and over (and to a lesser extent those for ages 85–94 years), the death rates were calculated using data from the 1990 census of population and deaths occurring in the United States to residents of Arizona in the 3 years 1989–91. Other publications in this decennial series present life tables for the United States and the other individual States. Generally, these reports show life tables calculated for the white population, the population other than white, and the black population separately by sex and for both sexes combined. Each of these reports also shows life tables for the total population, for total males, and for total females. Standard errors of the probability of dying and of life expectancy are also provided. However, life tables for the population other than white and for the black population in a State are not published when the total number of deaths for either males or females during the 3-year period is less than 700.

These life tables are the most recent in a series for the States that began with the 1939–41 period. Each of the tables in the series is based on a census of population and deaths in a 3-year period centered on the census year. Because State life tables are not currently produced on an annual basis, the decennial life tables are the only source of State life expectancy data available at the National Center for Health Statistics (NCHS).

Keywords: Arizona • decennial life tables • 1989–91 • life expectancy

This report is 1 of 51 reports containing life tables for the individual States and the District of Columbia. A separate report describes the methods and formulas by which these life tables were prepared in *U.S. Decennial Life Tables for 1989–91, Volume I, Number 2, Methodology of the National and State Life Tables* (1).

Methodology

The general methodology, with a few modifications, used in preparing these life tables was developed by Thomas N.E. Greville for the 1939–41 decennial life tables (2). The life tables are based on a complete count of deaths to residents of Arizona that occurred anywhere in the United States during the 3 years of 1989, 1990, and 1991 and on the 1990 census of population for Arizona. However, sometimes the observed death rates that these data produced did not meet certain well-established criteria, such as steadily increasing mortality with increasing age. For example, when the pattern of age-specific death rates at some ages was jagged rather than smooth or when the rates by race or sex were inconsistent, the observed death rates were adjusted slightly by moving deaths from one age group to another within the race-sex group. The total number of deaths in a race-sex group was never changed. Certain other adjustments were made. In accordance with standard practice, deaths for which age was not stated were allocated proportionately among the various age groups.

The population data used differ from the official data published by the U.S. Bureau of the Census because of age reporting problems in the 1990 census. Age was based on the respondents' direct reports of age at last birthday in the 1990 census. It was apparent that many respondents had reported their age at either the time of completion of the census form or at the time of the interview by an enumerator, which could have occurred several months after the April 1 reference date. As a result, reported age was biased upward and had to be modified.

Between the ages of 5 and 94 years, death rates were calculated using the total number of deaths in 1989–91 and 3 times the population shown in the 1990 census. However, since population counts at ages under 2 years are considered to be less reliable than those at other ages, life-table values at ages under 2 years were derived from the reported numbers of births for each of the years 1987 to 1991. At ages 2–4 years, the denominator of the death rates used the populations at ages x−1, x, and x+1 (instead of 3 times the population at age x). Death rates at ages 95 years and over, where the data from the census and from registered deaths are scanty and the accuracy of the reporting of age is not as good as at younger ages, are based on data from the Medicare program. However, when the data from the Medicare program were judged to be unreliable (usually after age 97), an algorithm was used to produce the death rates. The new algorithm, which differed from the one used for the 1979–81 decennial life tables, incremented the death rates more rapidly resulting in lower life expectancies at the extreme ages than in the previous reports. The rates based on the Medicare program and on the algorithm are differentiated by race and sex but not by State, so the same rates are used for each State. As a consequence, the probabilities of dying and the life expectancies at ages 85 years and over may fail to adequately reflect variation in mortality among the States, but such variation is in general smaller than differences associated with race and sex. Death rates at ages 85–94 years were adjusted to provide a smooth transition between the death rates based on the census and registered deaths and those derived from the Medicare program.

The population and death statistics at ages under 85 years are known to be subject to reporting errors, but these were not considered to be serious enough to require adjustment prior to the calculation of the life tables. In some instances, fluctuations due to small numbers of deaths produced anomalous life-tables values, which were eliminated by minor redistribution of deaths by age. For a complete description of the methodology used in preparing these life tables, see *U.S. Decennial Life Tables for 1989–91, Volume I, Number 2, Methodology of the National and State Life Tables* (1).

Results and discussion

The life tables in this report are current life tables and are based on age-specific death rates for the period 1989–91. They may also be characterized as "cross-sectional." They assume that a hypothetical cohort is traced from birth until the death of the last survivor and that it is subject throughout its existence to the age-specific death rates observed for 1989–91. For example, table 3 is a life table for females. This table shows the progression of a cohort starting with 100,000 live births who were subjected to the average annual death rates observed among females in Arizona in the 3-year period 1989–91 during its passage through successive years of age.

Column 7 of table 3 shows the average number of years of life remaining to those in the cohort who attain each birthday. This average remaining lifetime is commonly called the expectation of life, and the expectation of life at birth is frequently used as a measure of comparative longevity. According to the 1989–91 life tables for Arizona, the expectation of life at birth is 72.66 years for total males and 79.58 for total females. Among the 50 States and the District of Columbia in the expectation of life at birth for the total population, Arizona ranks 22d.

The ranking table shows the average lifetime (or expectation of life at birth) by race and sex for the population of the

United States, each State, and the District of Columbia. The States are ranked using the life expectancy at birth for the total population of the State.

These life tables are based on a complete count of resident deaths in Arizona during the 3 years 1989, 1990, and 1991. As such, they are not subject to sampling error. However, even complete counts may be considered as one of a large series of possible results that could have arisen under the same circumstances. This type of variation is known as random error. The standard errors shown in this report reflect random error only, not other errors such as misreporting of age on death certificates or in the census.

The probabilities of dying and the expectation of life presented in this report are "point estimates." They do not give the reader an indication of how accurate they are. Therefore standard errors of these two measures are also presented. Standard errors can be used to develop confidence intervals within which the "point estimates" are believed to lie. Standard errors of the probability of dying and of life expectancy contain six and three decimal places, respectively, and are shown in tables 13 and 14. In both cases, the standard errors contain one place more than the corresponding variable in the life tables. In computing confidence intervals, the limits are rounded to the same number of decimal places that the variable has in the life table.

Even though 68-percent confidence intervals are rarely used because of their high degree of uncertainty, they are shown here to demonstrate the method of construction of confidence intervals. To obtain a 68-percent confidence interval for the probability of dying at any age, take the point estimate from column 2 of the appropriate life table and add and subtract one standard error from the table that gives the standard errors of the probability of dying (table 13). The 95-percent confidence interval is obtained by adding and subtracting two standard errors. For example, the probability that a 50-year-old white female will die before her 51st birthday is 0.00317 with a standard error of 0.000259. Therefore, the 68-percent confidence interval is from 0.00291 to 0.00343 and the 95-percent confidence interval is from 0.00265 to 0.00369. The life expectancy of a 50-year-old white female is 32.25 years with a standard error of 0.055 years. The 68-percent confidence interval for the life expectancy is therefore from 32.20 to 32.31 years and the 95- percent confidence interval is from 32.14 to 32.36 years.

Explanation of the columns of the life table

Column 1—Age interval (x to x+1)—The age interval shown in column 1 is the interval of 1 year between the two exact ages indicated. For instance, "21–22" indicates the interval between the 21st birthday and the 22d, in other words, the 22d year of life.

Column 2—Proportion dying (q_x)—This column shows the proportion of the members of the life-table cohort alive at the beginning of the indicated year of age who will die before reaching the next birthday on the basis of the mortality rates of

1989–91 in Arizona. For example, for females who reach age 21, the proportion dying before reaching their 22d birthday is 0.00064—out of every 1,000 female babies surviving to age 21, 0.64 will die before reaching their 22d birthday.

Column 3—Number surviving (l_x)—This column shows the number of persons, starting with a cohort of 100,000 live births, who will survive to the birthday marking the beginning of the indicated year of age. Thus out of 100,000 female babies born alive in the cohort of table 3, 99,216 will complete the first year of life and enter the second, 98,544 will reach age 21, and 71,550 will live to age 75.

Column 4—Number dying (d_x)—This column shows the number dying in each successive age interval out of 100,000 live births. Thus out of 100,000 females born alive, 784 will die in the first year of life, 63 in the 22d year, and 2,046 in the 76th year. Each figure in column 4 is the difference between two successive figures in column 3.

Columns 5 and 6—Stationary population $(L_x$ and $T_x)$—Suppose that a group of 100,000 persons like that assumed in columns 3 and 4 is born every year, and that the proportion dying in each such group in each age interval throughout the lives of the members is exactly that shown in column 2. If there were no migration and if the births were evenly distributed over the year, the survivors of these births would constitute what is called a stationary population, because in such a population the number of persons living in any given age interval would never change. When an individual left an age interval, whether by death or growing older and entering the next higher age interval, his place would immediately be taken by someone entering from the next lower age interval. Thus a census taken at any time in such a stationary community would always show the same total population and the same numerical distribution of that population among the various age intervals. In such a stationary population supported by 100,000 annual births, column 3 shows the number of persons who, each year, will reach the exact age that marks the beginning of the age interval indicated in column 1, and column 4 shows the number of persons who will die each year in that year of age interval.

Column 5, L_x, shows the number of females in the stationary population in the indicated year of age. For example, the figure shown in table 3 for the year of age 21–22 is 98,513.

This means that in a stationary population supported by 100,000 annual births, and with proportions dying in each age interval always in accordance with column 2, a census taken on any date would show 98,513 persons at age 21 (that is, between exact ages 21 and 22 years).

Column 6, T_x, shows the total number of persons in the stationary population in the indicated year of age and all subsequent years of age. For example, in the stationary population of females described in the preceding paragraph, column 6 shows that there would be at any given moment a total of 5,881,040 persons who had reached their 21st birthday. The population at all ages 0 and above (in other words, the total female population of the stationary community) would be 7,958,343.

Column 7—Average remaining lifetime $(\overset{\circ}{e}_x)$—The average remaining lifetime (also called expectation of life) at any given age is the average number of years remaining to be lived by those surviving to that age, on the basis of a given set of age-specific rates of dying. In order to relate these figures to the preceding columns of the life table, it is necessary to observe that the figures in column 5 of the life tables can also be interpreted in terms of a single life-table cohort without introducing the concept of the stationary population. From this point of view, each figure in column 5 represents the total time in years lived between two indicated birthdays by all those reaching the younger age among the survivors of a cohort of 100,000 live births. Thus the figure of 98,513 for females in Arizona in the year of age 21–22 is the total number of years of life lived between their 21st and 22d birthdays by the 98,544 (column 3) who reached their 21st birthday out of the original cohort of 100,000 females born alive. The corresponding figure (5,881,040) in column 6 is the total number of years lived after attaining age 21 by the 98,544 reaching that exact age. This number of years divided by the number of persons (5,881,040 divided by 98,544) gives 59.68 years as the average remaining lifetime at age 21 for females in Arizona.

References

1. U.S. decennial life tables for 1989–91, volume I, number 2, methodology of the national and State life tables. In progress.
2. Greville TNE. United States life tables and actuarial tables, 1939–41. Washington: U.S. Government Printing Office. 1947.

Average lifetime in years by race and sex: United States and each State in rank order, 1989–91

Rank	Area	Total Both sexes	Total Male	Total Female	White Both sexes	White Male	White Female	All other Total Both sexes	All other Total Male	All other Total Female	Black Both sexes	Black Male	Black Female
1	Hawaii	78.21	75.37	81.26	77.92	75.12	81.09	78.40	75.49	81.48	*	*	*
2	Minnesota	77.76	74.53	80.85	77.97	74.78	81.02	73.05	69.46	76.80	*	*	*
3	Utah	77.70	74.93	80.38	77.77	75.00	80.44	*	*	*	*	*	*
4	North Dakota	77.62	74.35	80.99	77.99	74.74	81.32	*	*	*	*	*	*
5	Iowa	77.29	73.89	80.54	77.38	73.98	80.62	*	*	*	*	*	*
6	Colorado	76.96	73.79	80.01	77.06	73.88	80.13	75.71	72.63	78.61	72.41	68.96	75.89
7	Nebraska	76.92	73.57	80.17	77.21	73.87	80.44	71.14	67.64	74.52	*	*	*
8	Connecticut	76.91	73.62	79.97	77.44	74.25	80.37	72.31	67.82	76.61	70.84	66.04	75.44
8	South Dakota	76.91	73.17	80.77	77.91	74.30	81.59	*	*	*	*	*	*
10	Idaho	76.88	73.88	79.93	76.89	73.90	79.93	*	*	*	*	*	*
11	Wisconsin	76.87	73.61	80.03	77.18	73.99	80.27	72.37	68.27	76.25	70.96	66.42	75.27
12	Washington	76.82	73.84	79.74	76.92	73.97	79.81	76.09	72.72	79.59	71.34	67.91	75.58
13	Kansas	76.76	73.40	79.99	77.06	73.72	80.25	72.77	69.25	76.26	71.22	67.48	75.04
14	Massachusetts	76.72	73.32	79.80	76.90	73.54	79.95	75.08	71.29	78.60	72.45	68.17	76.50
14	New Hampshire	76.72	73.52	79.77	76.68	73.48	79.74	*	*	*	*	*	*
16	Rhode Island	76.54	73.00	79.77	76.80	73.31	79.97	*	*	*	*	*	*
16	Vermont	76.54	73.29	79.68	76.50	73.25	79.65	*	*	*	*	*	*
18	Oregon	76.44	73.21	79.67	76.51	73.28	79.73	75.24	72.02	78.45	*	*	*
19	Maine	76.35	72.98	79.61	76.35	72.98	79.61	*	*	*	*	*	*
20	Montana	76.23	73.05	79.49	76.72	73.59	79.92	*	*	*	*	*	*
21	Wyoming	76.21	73.16	79.29	76.34	73.27	79.46	*	*	*	*	*	*
22	Arizona	76.10	72.66	79.58	76.42	73.04	79.84	72.76	68.89	76.81	70.84	67.20	74.90
23	California	75.86	72.53	79.19	75.92	72.61	79.26	75.79	72.34	79.18	69.65	65.43	74.07
24	Florida	75.84	72.10	79.60	76.82	73.19	80.46	69.82	65.40	74.19	68.77	64.26	73.28
25	New Mexico	75.74	72.20	79.33	76.08	72.66	79.53	73.41	68.97	77.93	*	*	*
26	New Jersey	75.42	72.16	78.49	76.46	73.37	79.34	70.73	66.59	74.66	68.47	63.87	72.88
27	Indiana	75.39	71.99	78.62	75.82	72.44	79.03	70.76	66.99	74.35	69.80	65.87	73.56
28	Pennsylvania	75.38	71.91	78.66	76.15	72.81	79.28	69.34	64.69	73.78	68.27	63.33	73.02
	United States	75.37	71.83	78.81	76.13	72.72	79.45	71.25	66.97	75.39	69.16	64.47	73.73
29	Ohio	75.32	71.99	78.45	75.93	72.70	78.95	70.86	66.70	74.82	70.15	65.80	74.29
30	Missouri	75.25	71.54	78.82	76.02	72.43	79.48	69.65	65.00	74.07	68.81	63.87	73.52
31	Virginia	75.22	71.77	78.56	76.34	73.04	79.48	71.17	67.03	75.27	70.05	65.75	74.37
32	Texas	75.14	71.41	78.87	75.75	72.08	79.42	71.25	67.08	75.38	69.79	65.36	74.23
33	Oklahoma	75.10	71.63	78.49	75.21	71.76	78.59	74.81	71.17	78.21	70.85	67.10	74.48
34	Michigan	75.04	71.71	78.24	76.18	73.06	79.14	69.22	64.68	73.65	68.49	63.68	73.18
35	Illinois	74.90	71.34	78.31	76.16	72.83	79.33	69.25	64.58	73.79	67.46	62.41	72.39
36	Alaska	74.83	71.60	78.60	75.83	72.82	79.40	71.67	67.65	76.17	*	*	*
37	Maryland	74.79	71.31	78.13	76.30	73.20	79.23	70.76	66.27	75.15	69.69	64.99	74.31
38	Delaware	74.76	71.63	77.74	75.76	72.75	78.62	70.06	66.39	73.63	69.26	65.51	72.91
39	New York	74.68	70.86	78.32	75.61	72.01	79.03	71.53	66.70	75.97	69.33	63.86	74.35
40	North Carolina	74.48	70.58	78.27	75.89	72.21	79.44	69.83	64.96	74.55	69.38	64.38	74.24
41	Kentucky	74.37	70.72	77.97	74.65	71.01	78.24	70.79	66.78	74.63	70.16	66.06	74.13
42	Arkansas	74.33	70.54	78.13	75.20	71.54	78.89	69.63	64.87	74.13	68.93	64.03	73.58
43	Tennessee	74.32	70.38	78.18	75.27	71.38	79.10	69.43	64.99	73.59	68.97	64.41	73.24
44	West Virginia	74.26	70.53	77.93	74.37	70.66	78.02	71.20	66.77	75.46	69.75	65.00	74.36
45	Nevada	74.18	70.96	77.76	74.44	71.26	77.99	72.74	69.15	76.42	*	*	*
46	Alabama	73.64	69.59	77.61	75.01	71.12	78.85	69.59	64.79	74.05	69.23	64.37	73.76
47	Georgia	73.61	69.65	77.46	75.24	71.46	78.94	69.21	64.49	73.65	68.79	63.98	73.34
48	South Carolina	73.51	69.59	77.34	75.33	71.62	78.97	69.09	64.37	73.57	68.82	64.07	73.35
49	Louisiana	73.05	69.10	76.93	74.87	71.15	78.54	68.99	64.33	73.43	68.62	63.84	73.16
50	Mississippi	73.03	68.90	77.10	74.78	70.74	78.82	69.54	64.84	73.91	69.41	64.66	73.82
51	District Of Columbia	67.99	61.97	74.23	76.09	71.36	81.06	64.97	58.14	72.03	64.44	57.53	71.61

* Figure does not meet standards of reliability and precision.

Detailed tables

Table 1. Life table for the total population: Arizona, 1989–91

Age in years Period of life between two exact ages stated (1) x to x+1	Proportion dying Proportion of persons alive at beginning of year of age dying during year (2) q_x	Of 100,000 born alive		Stationary population		Average remaining lifetime Average number of years of life remaining at beginning of year of age (7) $\overset{\circ}{e}_x$
		Number living at beginning of year of age (3) l_x	Number dying during year of age (4) d_x	In year of age (5) L_x	In this year of age and all subsequent years (6) T_x	
0–1	.00891	100,000	891	99,309	7,609,557	76.10
1–2	.00082	99,109	81	99,068	7,510,248	75.78
2–3	.00060	99,028	60	98,998	7,411,180	74.84
3–4	.00046	98,968	46	98,945	7,312,182	73.88
4–5	.00037	98,922	36	98,905	7,213,237	72.92
5–6	.00031	98,886	31	98,870	7,114,332	71.94
6–7	.00027	98,855	27	98,842	7,015,462	70.97
7–8	.00024	98,828	23	98,817	6,916,620	69.99
8–9	.00020	98,805	20	98,794	6,817,803	69.00
9–10	.00017	98,785	17	98,777	6,719,009	68.02
10–11	.00015	98,768	14	98,761	6,620,232	67.03
11–12	.00015	98,754	15	98,746	6,521,471	66.04
12–13	.00021	98,739	21	98,728	6,422,725	65.05
13–14	.00032	98,718	31	98,703	6,323,997	64.06
14–15	.00048	98,687	48	98,663	6,225,294	63.08
15–16	.00065	98,639	64	98,607	6,126,631	62.11
16–17	.00082	98,575	81	98,534	6,028,024	61.15
17–18	.00095	98,494	94	98,447	5,929,490	60.20
18–19	.00105	98,400	103	98,349	5,831,043	59.26
19–20	.00111	98,297	109	98,242	5,732,694	58.32
20–21	.00117	98,188	115	98,130	5,634,452	57.38
21–22	.00123	98,073	121	98,012	5,536,322	56.45
22–23	.00126	97,952	123	97,891	5,438,310	55.52
23–24	.00126	97,829	124	97,767	5,340,419	54.59
24–25	.00125	97,705	122	97,644	5,242,652	53.66
25–26	.00122	97,583	119	97,524	5,145,008	52.72
26–27	.00121	97,464	117	97,405	5,047,484	51.79
27–28	.00120	97,347	118	97,288	4,950,079	50.85
28–29	.00123	97,229	119	97,170	4,852,791	49.91
29–30	.00127	97,110	124	97,048	4,755,621	48.97
30–31	.00132	96,986	128	96,922	4,658,573	48.03
31–32	.00137	96,858	132	96,792	4,561,651	47.10
32–33	.00143	96,726	138	96,657	4,464,859	46.16
33–34	.00149	96,588	144	96,516	4,368,202	45.23
34–35	.00156	96,444	150	96,369	4,271,686	44.29
35–36	.00164	96,294	158	96,215	4,175,317	43.36
36–37	.00173	96,136	166	96,053	4,079,102	42.43
37–38	.00183	95,970	175	95,882	3,983,049	41.50
38–39	.00195	95,795	187	95,702	3,887,167	40.58
39–40	.00207	95,608	198	95,509	3,791,465	39.66
40–41	.00221	95,410	211	95,305	3,695,956	38.74
41–42	.00236	95,199	224	95,087	3,600,651	37.82
42–43	.00252	94,975	240	94,855	3,505,564	36.91
43–44	.00271	94,735	256	94,607	3,410,709	36.00
44–45	.00292	94,479	276	94,342	3,316,102	35.10
45–46	.00317	94,203	299	94,053	3,221,760	34.20
46–47	.00346	93,904	325	93,742	3,127,707	33.31
47–48	.00376	93,579	352	93,404	3,033,965	32.42
48–49	.00404	93,227	377	93,038	2,940,561	31.54
49–50	.00432	92,850	401	92,650	2,847,523	30.67
50–51	.00463	92,449	428	92,235	2,754,873	29.80
51–52	.00501	92,021	461	91,791	2,662,638	28.94
52–53	.00547	91,560	501	91,310	2,570,847	28.08
53–54	.00603	91,059	548	90,785	2,479,537	27.23
54–55	.00667	90,511	604	90,209	2,388,752	26.39

Table 1. Life table for the total population: Arizona, 1989–91—Con.

Age in years	Proportion dying	Of 100,000 born alive		Stationary population		Average remaining lifetime
Period of life between two exact ages stated (1)	Proporion of persons alive at beginning of year of age dying during year (2)	Number living at beginning of year of age (3)	Number dying during year of age (4)	In year of age (5)	In this year of age and all subsequent years (6)	Average number of years of life remaining at beginning of year of age (7)
x to $x+1$	q_x	l_x	d_x	L_x	T_x	$\overset{\circ}{e}_x$
55–56	.00737	89,907	663	89,575	2,298,543	25.57
56–57	.00812	89,244	725	88,882	2,208,968	24.75
57–58	.00891	88,519	788	88,125	2,120,086	23.95
58–59	.00972	87,731	853	87,304	2,031,961	23.16
59–60	.01056	86,878	917	86,420	1,944,657	22.38
60–61	.01139	85,961	979	85,471	1,858,237	21.62
61–62	.01227	84,982	1,043	84,461	1,772,766	20.86
62–63	.01323	83,939	1,110	83,384	1,688,305	20.11
63–64	.01429	82,829	1,184	82,236	1,604,921	19.38
64–65	.01543	81,645	1,260	81,016	1,522,685	18.65
65–66	.01654	80,385	1,329	79,720	1,441,669	17.93
66–67	.01767	79,056	1,397	78,357	1,361,949	17.23
67–68	.01895	77,659	1,472	76,923	1,283,592	16.53
68–69	.02050	76,187	1,562	75,406	1,206,669	15.84
69–70	.02236	74,625	1,668	73,791	1,131,263	15.16
70–71	.02447	72,957	1,786	72,064	1,057,472	14.49
71–72	.02676	71,171	1,904	70,219	985,408	13.85
72–73	.02922	69,267	2,024	68,255	915,189	13.21
73–74	.03180	67,243	2,139	66,174	846,934	12.60
74–75	.03447	65,104	2,244	63,982	780,760	11.99
75–76	.03737	62,860	2,349	61,685	716,778	11.40
76–77	.04058	60,511	2,456	59,283	655,093	10.83
77–78	.04412	58,055	2,561	56,775	595,810	10.26
78–79	.04805	55,494	2,666	54,161	539,035	9.71
79–80	.05249	52,828	2,774	51,441	484,874	9.18
80–81	.05766	50,054	2,886	48,612	433,433	8.66
81–82	.06352	47,168	2,996	45,670	384,821	8.16
82–83	.06983	44,172	3,084	42,630	339,151	7.68
83–84	.07629	41,088	3,135	39,520	296,521	7.22
84–85	.08296	37,953	3,149	36,379	257,001	6.77
85–86	.09123	34,804	3,175	33,217	220,622	6.34
86–87	.10100	31,629	3,195	30,032	187,405	5.93
87–88	.11178	28,434	3,178	26,845	157,373	5.53
88–89	.12337	25,256	3,116	23,698	130,528	5.17
89–90	.13583	22,140	3,007	20,637	106,830	4.83
90–91	.14981	19,133	2,867	17,700	86,193	4.50
91–92	.16537	16,266	2,690	14,921	68,493	4.21
92–93	.18121	13,576	2,460	12,347	53,572	3.95
93–94	.19626	11,116	2,181	10,025	41,225	3.71
94–95	.21052	8,935	1,881	7,994	31,200	3.49
95–96	.22502	7,054	1,588	6,260	23,206	3.29
96–97	.24126	5,466	1,318	4,807	16,946	3.10
97–98	.25689	4,148	1,066	3,615	12,139	2.93
98–99	.27175	3,082	837	2,663	8,524	2.77
99–100	.28751	2,245	646	1,922	5,861	2.61
100–101	.30418	1,599	486	1,356	3,939	2.46
101–102	.32182	1,113	358	934	2,583	2.32
102–103	.34049	755	257	626	1,649	2.19
103–104	.36024	498	180	408	1,023	2.05
104–105	.38113	318	121	258	615	1.93
105–106	.40324	197	79	157	357	1.81
106–107	.42663	118	51	93	200	1.70
107–108	.45137	67	30	52	107	1.59
108–109	.47755	37	18	28	55	1.49
109–110	.50525	19	9	15	27	1.39

3–5

Table 2. Life table for males: Arizona, 1989–91

Age in years	Proportion dying	Of 100,000 born alive		Stationary population		Average remaining lifetime
Period of life between two exact ages stated (1)	Proportion of persons alive at beginning of year of age dying during year (2)	Number living at beginning of year of age (3)	Number dying during year of age (4)	In year of age (5)	In this year of age and all subsequent years (6)	Average number of years of life remaining at beginning of year of age (7)
x to x+1	q_x	l_x	d_x	L_x	T_x	$\overset{\circ}{e}_x$
0–1	.00993	100,000	993	99,240	7,266,244	72.66
1–2	.00092	99,007	91	98,961	7,167,004	72.39
2–3	.00071	98,916	70	98,881	7,068,043	71.46
3–4	.00052	98,846	51	98,820	6,969,162	70.51
4–5	.00042	98,795	42	98,774	6,870,342	69.54
5–6	.00035	98,753	35	98,735	6,771,568	68.57
6–7	.00031	98,718	31	98,703	6,672,833	67.59
7–8	.00027	98,687	27	98,674	6,574,130	66.62
8–9	.00023	98,660	23	98,648	6,475,456	65.63
9–10	.00019	98,637	19	98,628	6,376,808	64.65
10–11	.00016	98,618	15	98,611	6,278,180	63.66
11–12	.00016	98,603	16	98,595	6,179,569	62.67
12–13	.00025	98,587	25	98,574	6,080,974	61.68
13–14	.00043	98,562	42	98,542	5,982,400	60.70
14–15	.00068	98,520	66	98,486	5,883,858	59.72
15–16	.00095	98,454	94	98,407	5,785,372	58.76
16–17	.00120	98,360	117	98,302	5,686,965	57.82
17–18	.00140	98,243	138	98,174	5,588,663	56.89
18–19	.00154	98,105	151	98,029	5,490,489	55.97
19–20	.00162	97,954	158	97,875	5,392,460	55.05
20–21	.00169	97,796	166	97,713	5,294,585	54.14
21–22	.00177	97,630	173	97,544	5,196,872	53.23
22–23	.00181	97,457	176	97,369	5,099,328	52.32
23–24	.00182	97,281	178	97,192	5,001,959	51.42
24–25	.00181	97,103	175	97,016	4,904,767	50.51
25–26	.00178	96,928	173	96,841	4,807,751	49.60
26–27	.00176	96,755	171	96,669	4,710,910	48.69
27–28	.00177	96,584	171	96,499	4,614,241	47.77
28–29	.00181	96,413	175	96,325	4,517,742	46.86
29–30	.00188	96,238	181	96,148	4,421,417	45.94
30–31	.00197	96,057	189	95,963	4,325,269	45.03
31–32	.00204	95,868	196	95,770	4,229,306	44.12
32–33	.00212	95,672	203	95,570	4,133,536	43.21
33–34	.00220	95,469	210	95,364	4,037,966	42.30
34–35	.00228	95,259	218	95,150	3,942,602	41.39
35–36	.00237	95,041	225	94,928	3,847,452	40.48
36–37	.00248	94,816	235	94,699	3,752,524	39.58
37–38	.00260	94,581	246	94,457	3,657,825	38.67
38–39	.00276	94,335	261	94,205	3,563,368	37.77
39–40	.00293	94,074	276	93,936	3,469,163	36.88
40–41	.00313	93,798	293	93,652	3,375,227	35.98
41–42	.00333	93,505	312	93,349	3,281,575	35.10
42–43	.00354	93,193	329	93,029	3,188,226	34.21
43–44	.00375	92,864	348	92,690	3,095,197	33.33
44–45	.00397	92,516	367	92,332	3,002,507	32.45
45–46	.00423	92,149	390	91,954	2,910,175	31.58
46–47	.00455	91,759	418	91,550	2,818,221	30.71
47–48	.00489	91,341	446	91,118	2,726,671	29.85
48–49	.00524	90,895	477	90,657	2,635,553	29.00
49–50	.00561	90,418	507	90,164	2,544,896	28.15
50–51	.00603	89,911	542	89,640	2,454,732	27.30
51–52	.00653	89,369	583	89,078	2,365,092	26.46
52–53	.00714	88,786	634	88,469	2,276,014	25.63
53–54	.00787	88,152	694	87,805	2,187,545	24.82
54–55	.00871	87,458	762	87,077	2,099,740	24.01

Table 2. Life table for males: Arizona, 1989–91—Con.

Age in years	Proportion dying	Of 100,000 born alive		Stationary population		Average remaining lifetime
Period of life between two exact ages stated (1)	Proportion of persons alive at beginning of year of age dying during year (2)	Number living at beginning of year of age (3)	Number dying during year of age (4)	In year of age (5)	In this year of age and all subsequent years (6)	Average number of years of life remaining at beginning of year of age (7)
x to $x+1$	q_x	l_x	d_x	L_x	T_x	$\overset{\circ}{e}_x$
55–56	.00963	86,696	834	86,279	2,012,663	23.22
56–57	.01060	85,862	910	85,407	1,926,384	22.44
57–58	.01161	84,952	987	84,458	1,840,977	21.67
58–59	.01267	83,965	1,064	83,434	1,756,519	20.92
59–60	.01376	82,901	1,141	82,330	1,673,085	20.18
60–61	.01487	81,760	1,215	81,153	1,590,755	19.46
61–62	.01603	80,545	1,292	79,899	1,509,602	18.74
62–63	.01730	79,253	1,371	78,567	1,429,703	18.04
63–64	.01869	77,882	1,456	77,155	1,351,136	17.35
64–65	.02017	76,426	1,541	75,655	1,273,981	16.67
65–66	.02160	74,885	1,617	74,077	1,198,326	16.00
66–67	.02305	73,268	1,689	72,423	1,124,249	15.34
67–68	.02472	71,579	1,770	70,694	1,051,826	14.69
68–69	.02678	69,809	1,869	68,874	981,132	14.05
69–70	.02924	67,940	1,987	66,947	912,258	13.43
70–71	.03201	65,953	2,112	64,897	845,311	12.82
71–72	.03495	63,841	2,231	62,726	780,414	12.22
72–73	.03809	61,610	2,346	60,436	717,688	11.65
73–74	.04133	59,264	2,450	58,039	657,252	11.09
74–75	.04471	56,814	2,540	55,544	599,213	10.55
75–76	.04843	54,274	2,629	52,959	543,669	10.02
76–77	.05258	51,645	2,715	50,288	490,710	9.50
77–78	.05703	48,930	2,791	47,534	440,422	9.00
78–79	.06177	46,139	2,850	44,715	392,888	8.52
79–80	.06692	43,289	2,896	41,841	348,173	8.04
80–81	.07296	40,393	2,947	38,919	306,332	7.58
81–82	.07997	37,446	2,995	35,949	267,413	7.14
82–83	.08740	34,451	3,011	32,945	231,464	6.72
83–84	.09469	31,440	2,977	29,952	198,519	6.31
84–85	.10182	28,463	2,898	27,015	168,567	5.92
85–86	.11126	25,565	2,844	24,143	141,552	5.54
86–87	.12256	22,721	2,785	21,328	117,409	5.17
87–88	.13512	19,936	2,694	18,589	96,081	4.82
88–89	.14879	17,242	2,565	15,960	77,492	4.49
89–90	.16350	14,677	2,400	13,477	61,532	4.19
90–91	.17959	12,277	2,205	11,175	48,055	3.91
91–92	.19725	10,072	1,987	9,079	36,880	3.66
92–93	.21534	8,085	1,741	7,215	27,801	3.44
93–94	.23225	6,344	1,473	5,607	20,586	3.24
94–95	.24688	4,871	1,203	4,270	14,979	3.08
95–96	.26004	3,668	954	3,191	10,709	2.92
96–97	.27536	2,714	747	2,341	7,518	2.77
97–98	.28943	1,967	569	1,682	5,177	2.63
98–99	.30390	1,398	425	1,185	3,495	2.50
99–100	.31910	973	311	818	2,310	2.37
100–101	.33505	662	221	552	1,492	2.25
101–102	.35181	441	155	363	940	2.13
102–103	.36940	286	106	232	577	2.02
103–104	.38787	180	70	145	345	1.91
104–105	.40726	110	45	88	200	1.81
105–106	.42762	65	28	52	112	1.71
106–107	.44900	37	16	29	60	1.61
107–108	.47145	21	10	15	31	1.52
108–109	.49503	11	6	9	16	1.43
109–110	.51978	5	2	4	7	1.35

Table 3. Life table for females: Arizona, 1989–91

Age in years	Proportion dying	Of 100,000 born alive		Stationary population		Average remaining lifetime
Period of life between two exact ages stated (1)	Proportion of persons alive at beginning of year of age dying during year (2)	Number living at beginning of year of age (3)	Number dying during year of age (4)	In year of age (5)	In this year of age and all subsequent years (6)	Average number of years of life remaining at beginning of year of age (7)
x to $x+1$	q_x	l_x	d_x	L_x	T_x	$\overset{o}{e}_x$
0–1	.00784	100,000	784	99,383	7,958,343	79.58
1–2	.00072	99,216	71	99,180	7,858,960	79.21
2–3	.00050	99,145	49	99,120	7,759,780	78.27
3–4	.00040	99,096	40	99,076	7,660,660	77.31
4–5	.00031	99,056	30	99,042	7,561,584	76.34
5–6	.00027	99,026	27	99,012	7,462,542	75.36
6–7	.00023	98,999	23	98,988	7,363,530	74.38
7–8	.00020	98,976	19	98,967	7,264,542	73.40
8–9	.00017	98,957	17	98,948	7,165,575	72.41
9–10	.00015	98,940	15	98,933	7,066,627	71.42
10–11	.00014	98,925	13	98,918	6,967,694	70.43
11–12	.00014	98,912	14	98,905	6,868,776	69.44
12–13	.00016	98,898	16	98,890	6,769,871	68.45
13–14	.00021	98,882	21	98,871	6,670,981	67.46
14–15	.00027	98,861	27	98,848	6,572,110	66.48
15–16	.00035	98,834	34	98,817	6,473,262	65.50
16–17	.00042	98,800	41	98,780	6,374,445	64.52
17–18	.00048	98,759	48	98,735	6,275,665	63.55
18–19	.00053	98,711	52	98,685	6,176,930	62.58
19–20	.00057	98,659	56	98,632	6,078,245	61.61
20–21	.00060	98,603	59	98,573	5,979,613	60.64
21–22	.00064	98,544	63	98,513	5,881,040	59.68
22–23	.00066	98,481	65	98,448	5,782,527	58.72
23–24	.00066	98,416	65	98,383	5,684,079	57.76
24–25	.00065	98,351	64	98,319	5,585,696	56.79
25–26	.00063	98,287	62	98,256	5,487,377	55.83
26–27	.00062	98,225	61	98,195	5,389,121	54.86
27–28	.00062	98,164	60	98,134	5,290,926	53.90
28–29	.00062	98,104	61	98,074	5,192,792	52.93
29–30	.00064	98,043	63	98,011	5,094,718	51.96
30–31	.00066	97,980	65	97,947	4,996,707	51.00
31–32	.00068	97,915	66	97,882	4,898,760	50.03
32–33	.00071	97,849	70	97,814	4,800,878	49.06
33–34	.00076	97,779	75	97,742	4,703,064	48.10
34–35	.00082	97,704	80	97,664	4,605,322	47.14
35–36	.00089	97,624	87	97,581	4,507,658	46.17
36–37	.00097	97,537	95	97,489	4,410,077	45.21
37–38	.00105	97,442	103	97,391	4,312,588	44.26
38–39	.00113	97,339	110	97,285	4,215,197	43.30
39–40	.00121	97,229	117	97,170	4,117,912	42.35
40–41	.00129	97,112	125	97,050	4,020,742	41.40
41–42	.00138	96,987	134	96,920	3,923,692	40.46
42–43	.00151	96,853	146	96,780	3,826,772	39.51
43–44	.00167	96,707	161	96,626	3,729,992	38.57
44–45	.00188	96,546	182	96,455	3,633,366	37.63
45–46	.00214	96,364	206	96,261	3,536,911	36.70
46–47	.00241	96,158	232	96,042	3,440,650	35.78
47–48	.00268	95,926	257	95,798	3,344,608	34.87
48–49	.00290	95,669	277	95,531	3,248,810	33.96
49–50	.00310	95,392	296	95,244	3,153,279	33.06
50–51	.00331	95,096	314	94,939	3,058,035	32.16
51–52	.00358	94,782	340	94,612	2,963,096	31.26
52–53	.00391	94,442	369	94,257	2,868,484	30.37
53–54	.00431	94,073	405	93,871	2,774,227	29.49
54–55	.00477	93,668	446	93,445	2,680,356	28.62

Table 3. Life table for females: Arizona, 1989–91—Con.

Age in years	Proportion dying	Of 100,000 born alive		Stationary population		Average remaining lifetime
Period of life between two exact ages stated (1)	Proportion of persons alive at beginning of year of age dying during year (2)	Number living at beginning of year of age (3)	Number dying during year of age (4)	In year of age (5)	In this year of age and all subsequent years (6)	Average number of years of life remaining at beginning of year of age (7)
x to $x+1$	q_x	l_x	d_x	L_x	T_x	$\overset{\circ}{e}_x$
55–56	.00527	93,222	492	92,976	2,586,911	27.75
56–57	.00582	92,730	539	92,460	2,493,935	26.89
57–58	.00641	92,191	591	91,896	2,401,475	26.05
58–59	.00703	91,600	643	91,278	2,309,579	25.21
59–60	.00767	90,957	698	90,608	2,218,301	24.39
60–61	.00831	90,259	749	89,884	2,127,693	23.57
61–62	.00897	89,510	803	89,108	2,037,809	22.77
62–63	.00970	88,707	861	88,277	1,948,701	21.97
63–64	.01052	87,846	924	87,383	1,860,424	21.18
64–65	.01140	86,922	991	86,427	1,773,041	20.40
65–66	.01227	85,931	1,055	85,403	1,686,614	19.63
66–67	.01316	84,876	1,117	84,318	1,601,211	18.87
67–68	.01413	83,759	1,183	83,167	1,516,893	18.11
68–69	.01526	82,576	1,260	81,946	1,433,726	17.36
69–70	.01661	81,316	1,351	80,641	1,351,780	16.62
70–71	.01816	79,965	1,452	79,238	1,271,139	15.90
71–72	.01988	78,513	1,561	77,733	1,191,901	15.18
72–73	.02182	76,952	1,679	76,113	1,114,168	14.48
73–74	.02392	75,273	1,800	74,373	1,038,055	13.79
74–75	.02617	73,473	1,923	72,511	963,682	13.12
75–76	.02859	71,550	2,046	70,527	891,171	12.46
76–77	.03128	69,504	2,174	68,417	820,644	11.81
77–78	.03434	67,330	2,312	66,173	752,227	11.17
78–79	.03792	65,018	2,466	63,785	686,054	10.55
79–80	.04208	62,552	2,632	61,237	622,269	9.95
80–81	.04692	59,920	2,811	58,514	561,032	9.36
81–82	.05236	57,109	2,990	55,614	502,518	8.80
82–83	.05830	54,119	3,155	52,542	446,904	8.26
83–84	.06461	50,964	3,293	49,317	394,362	7.74
84–85	.07138	47,671	3,403	45,970	345,045	7.24
85–86	.07970	44,268	3,528	42,504	299,075	6.76
86–87	.08945	40,740	3,644	38,918	256,571	6.30
87–88	.10015	37,096	3,715	35,238	217,653	5.87
88–89	.11158	33,381	3,725	31,519	182,415	5.46
89–90	.12384	29,656	3,672	27,820	150,896	5.09
90–91	.13783	25,984	3,582	24,193	123,076	4.74
91–92	.15354	22,402	3,440	20,682	98,883	4.41
92–93	.16951	18,962	3,214	17,355	78,201	4.12
93–94	.18473	15,748	2,909	14,294	60,846	3.86
94–95	.19946	12,839	2,561	11,558	46,552	3.63
95–96	.21475	10,278	2,207	9,175	34,994	3.40
96–97	.23143	8,071	1,868	7,137	25,819	3.20
97–98	.24775	6,203	1,537	5,435	18,682	3.01
98–99	.26375	4,666	1,230	4,050	13,247	2.84
99–100	.27957	3,436	961	2,956	9,197	2.68
100–101	.29635	2,475	733	2,108	6,241	2.52
101–102	.31413	1,742	548	1,468	4,133	2.37
102–103	.33298	1,194	397	996	2,665	2.23
103–104	.35296	797	281	656	1,669	2.10
104–105	.37413	516	193	419	1,013	1.97
105–106	.39658	323	128	259	594	1.84
106–107	.42038	195	82	153	335	1.72
107–108	.44560	113	50	88	182	1.61
108–109	.47233	63	30	48	94	1.50
109–110	.50068	33	17	25	46	1.40

Table 4. Life table for the white population: Arizona, 1989–91

Age in years	Proportion dying	Of 100,000 born alive		Stationary population		Average remaining lifetime
Period of life between two exact ages stated (1)	Proportion of persons alive at beginning of year of age dying during year (2)	Number living at beginning of year of age (3)	Number dying during year of age (4)	In year of age (5)	In this year of age and all subsequent years (6)	Average number of years of life remaining at beginning of year of age (7)
x to x+1	q_x	l_x	d_x	L_x	T_x	$\overset{\circ}{e}_x$
0–1	.00820	100,000	820	99,358	7,642,360	76.42
1–2	.00075	99,180	74	99,143	7,543,002	76.05
2–3	.00056	99,106	56	99,078	7,443,859	75.11
3–4	.00043	99,050	42	99,029	7,344,781	74.15
4–5	.00034	99,008	34	98,991	7,245,752	73.18
5–6	.00029	98,974	29	98,960	7,146,761	72.21
6–7	.00025	98,945	25	98,932	7,047,801	71.23
7–8	.00022	98,920	21	98,910	6,948,869	70.25
8–9	.00019	98,899	19	98,889	6,849,959	69.26
9–10	.00015	98,880	15	98,873	6,751,070	68.28
10–11	.00013	98,865	13	98,858	6,652,197	67.29
11–12	.00013	98,852	13	98,846	6,553,339	66.29
12–13	.00018	98,839	18	98,829	6,454,493	65.30
13–14	.00030	98,821	30	98,806	6,355,664	64.32
14–15	.00045	98,791	44	98,770	6,256,858	63.33
15–16	.00062	98,747	61	98,716	6,158,088	62.36
16–17	.00078	98,686	77	98,647	6,059,372	61.40
17–18	.00091	98,609	90	98,564	5,960,725	60.45
18–19	.00100	98,519	98	98,470	5,862,161	59.50
19–20	.00106	98,421	104	98,369	5,763,691	58.56
20–21	.00111	98,317	110	98,262	5,665,322	57.62
21–22	.00117	98,207	114	98,151	5,567,060	56.69
22–23	.00119	98,093	117	98,034	5,468,909	55.75
23–24	.00119	97,976	117	97,917	5,370,875	54.82
24–25	.00117	97,859	115	97,801	5,272,958	53.88
25–26	.00114	97,744	111	97,689	5,175,157	52.95
26–27	.00112	97,633	110	97,578	5,077,468	52.01
27–28	.00112	97,523	109	97,469	4,979,890	51.06
28–29	.00114	97,414	111	97,358	4,882,421	50.12
29–30	.00119	97,303	116	97,245	4,785,063	49.18
30–31	.00124	97,187	121	97,127	4,687,818	48.23
31–32	.00130	97,066	126	97,003	4,590,691	47.29
32–33	.00135	96,940	131	96,875	4,493,688	46.36
33–34	.00141	96,809	137	96,740	4,396,813	45.42
34–35	.00147	96,672	142	96,601	4,300,073	44.48
35–36	.00154	96,530	149	96,456	4,203,472	43.55
36–37	.00162	96,381	156	96,303	4,107,016	42.61
37–38	.00172	96,225	165	96,143	4,010,713	41.68
38–39	.00183	96,060	175	95,972	3,914,570	40.75
39–40	.00195	95,885	187	95,791	3,818,598	39.82
40–41	.00209	95,698	200	95,598	3,722,807	38.90
41–42	.00223	95,498	213	95,392	3,627,209	37.98
42–43	.00239	95,285	228	95,170	3,531,817	37.07
43–44	.00257	95,057	244	94,935	3,436,647	36.15
44–45	.00277	94,813	263	94,681	3,341,712	35.25
45–46	.00301	94,550	284	94,409	3,247,031	34.34
46–47	.00328	94,266	310	94,111	3,152,622	33.44
47–48	.00357	93,956	335	93,789	3,058,511	32.55
48–49	.00384	93,621	359	93,441	2,964,722	31.67
49–50	.00411	93,262	383	93,070	2,871,281	30.79
50–51	.00441	92,879	410	92,674	2,778,211	29.91
51–52	.00479	92,469	443	92,247	2,685,537	29.04
52–53	.00525	92,026	484	91,784	2,593,290	28.18
53–54	.00580	91,542	531	91,277	2,501,506	27.33
54–55	.00644	91,011	585	90,718	2,410,229	26.48

Table 4. Life table for the white population: Arizona, 1989–91—Con.

Age in years	Proportion dying	Of 100,000 born alive		Stationary population		Average remaining lifetime
Period of life between two exact ages stated (1)	Proportion of persons alive at beginning of year of age dying during year (2)	Number living at beginning of year of age (3)	Number dying during year of age (4)	In year of age (5)	In this year of age and all subsequent years (6)	Average number of years of life remaining at beginning of year of age (7)
x to $x+1$	q_x	l_x	d_x	L_x	T_x	$\overset{\circ}{e}_x$
55–56	.00713	90,426	645	90,104	2,319,511	25.65
56–57	.00787	89,781	707	89,427	2,229,407	24.83
57–58	.00866	89,074	772	88,689	2,139,980	24.02
58–59	.00949	88,302	838	87,883	2,051,291	23.23
59–60	.01035	87,464	905	87,011	1,963,408	22.45
60–61	.01120	86,559	970	86,075	1,876,397	21.68
61–62	.01209	85,589	1,034	85,072	1,790,322	20.92
62–63	.01305	84,555	1,104	84,003	1,705,250	20.17
63–64	.01410	83,451	1,177	82,862	1,621,247	19.43
64–65	.01522	82,274	1,252	81,648	1,538,385	18.70
65–66	.01631	81,022	1,321	80,361	1,456,737	17.98
66–67	.01741	79,701	1,388	79,007	1,376,376	17.27
67–68	.01867	78,313	1,462	77,582	1,297,369	16.57
68–69	.02022	76,851	1,555	76,074	1,219,787	15.87
69–70	.02209	75,296	1,663	74,464	1,143,713	15.19
70–71	.02422	73,633	1,783	72,742	1,069,249	14.52
71–72	.02650	71,850	1,904	70,898	996,507	13.87
72–73	.02897	69,946	2,026	68,932	925,609	13.23
73–74	.03152	67,920	2,142	66,849	856,677	12.61
74–75	.03418	65,778	2,248	64,655	789,828	12.01
75–76	.03705	63,530	2,353	62,353	725,173	11.41
76–77	.04025	61,177	2,463	59,946	662,820	10.83
77–78	.04378	58,714	2,570	57,429	602,874	10.27
78–79	.04771	56,144	2,679	54,804	545,445	9.72
79–80	.05214	53,465	2,787	52,072	490,641	9.18
80–81	.05729	50,678	2,903	49,226	438,569	8.65
81–82	.06314	47,775	3,017	46,266	389,343	8.15
82–83	.06945	44,758	3,109	43,204	343,077	7.67
83–84	.07595	41,649	3,163	40,068	299,873	7.20
84–85	.08273	38,486	3,184	36,894	259,805	6.75
85–86	.09115	35,302	3,217	33,693	222,911	6.31
86–87	.10114	32,085	3,246	30,462	189,218	5.90
87–88	.11217	28,839	3,234	27,222	158,756	5.50
88–89	.12394	25,605	3,174	24,018	131,534	5.14
89–90	.13650	22,431	3,062	20,900	107,516	4.79
90–91	.15059	19,369	2,917	17,911	86,616	4.47
91–92	.16635	16,452	2,736	15,084	68,705	4.18
92–93	.18250	13,716	2,503	12,464	53,621	3.91
93–94	.19795	11,213	2,220	10,103	41,157	3.67
94–95	.21269	8,993	1,913	8,037	31,054	3.45
95–96	.22760	7,080	1,611	6,274	23,017	3.25
96–97	.24414	5,469	1,335	4,801	16,743	3.06
97–98	.26009	4,134	1,075	3,596	11,942	2.89
98–99	.27538	3,059	843	2,638	8,346	2.73
99–100	.29135	2,216	645	1,893	5,708	2.58
100–101	.30824	1,571	485	1,329	3,815	2.43
101–102	.32612	1,086	354	909	2,486	2.29
102–103	.34504	732	252	606	1,577	2.15
103–104	.36505	480	176	392	971	2.03
104–105	.38622	304	117	246	579	1.90
105–106	.40862	187	76	148	333	1.78
106–107	.43232	111	48	87	185	1.67
107–108	.45740	63	29	48	98	1.56
108–109	.48393	34	16	26	50	1.46
109–110	.51200	18	9	13	24	1.36

Table 5. Life table for white males: Arizona, 1989–91

Age in years	Proportion dying	Of 100,000 born alive		Stationary population		Average remaining lifetime
Period of life between two exact ages stated (1)	Proportion of persons alive at beginning of year of age dying during year (2)	Number living at beginning of year of age (3)	Number dying during year of age (4)	In year of age (5)	In this year of age and all subsequent years (6)	Average number of years of life remaining at beginning of year of age (7)
x to $x+1$	q_x	l_x	d_x	L_x	T_x	$\overset{\circ}{e}_x$
0–1	.00911	100,000	911	99,298	7,304,470	73.04
1–2	.00082	99,089	81	99,048	7,205,172	72.71
2–3	.00065	99,008	65	98,975	7,106,124	71.77
3–4	.00048	98,943	48	98,920	7,007,149	70.82
4–5	.00040	98,895	40	98,875	6,908,229	69.85
5–6	.00033	98,855	32	98,839	6,809,354	68.88
6–7	.00029	98,823	29	98,809	6,710,515	67.90
7–8	.00026	98,794	25	98,781	6,611,706	66.92
8–9	.00021	98,769	21	98,758	6,512,925	65.94
9–10	.00017	98,748	17	98,740	6,414,167	64.96
10–11	.00013	98,731	13	98,724	6,315,427	63.97
11–12	.00014	98,718	14	98,711	6,216,703	62.97
12–13	.00022	98,704	21	98,694	6,117,992	61.98
13–14	.00039	98,683	38	98,664	6,019,298	61.00
14–15	.00063	98,645	62	98,614	5,920,634	60.02
15–16	.00089	98,583	88	98,539	5,822,020	59.06
16–17	.00113	98,495	111	98,440	5,723,481	58.11
17–18	.00133	98,384	130	98,319	5,625,041	57.17
18–19	.00146	98,254	143	98,182	5,526,722	56.25
19–20	.00154	98,111	152	98,035	5,428,540	55.33
20–21	.00162	97,959	158	97,880	5,330,505	54.42
21–22	.00170	97,801	166	97,718	5,232,625	53.50
22–23	.00174	97,635	170	97,550	5,134,907	52.59
23–24	.00174	97,465	169	97,381	5,037,357	51.68
24–25	.00172	97,296	167	97,212	4,939,976	50.77
25–26	.00168	97,129	164	97,047	4,842,764	49.86
26–27	.00166	96,965	161	96,885	4,745,717	48.94
27–28	.00166	96,804	161	96,723	4,648,832	48.02
28–29	.00171	96,643	165	96,561	4,552,109	47.10
29–30	.00179	96,478	173	96,391	4,455,548	46.18
30–31	.00188	96,305	181	96,215	4,359,157	45.26
31–32	.00197	96,124	189	96,030	4,262,942	44.35
32–33	.00205	95,935	196	95,837	4,166,912	43.43
33–34	.00212	95,739	203	95,637	4,071,075	42.52
34–35	.00218	95,536	208	95,432	3,975,438	41.61
35–36	.00225	95,328	214	95,221	3,880,006	40.70
36–37	.00233	95,114	222	95,003	3,784,785	39.79
37–38	.00244	94,892	231	94,777	3,689,782	38.88
38–39	.00259	94,661	245	94,538	3,595,005	37.98
39–40	.00276	94,416	261	94,285	3,500,467	37.08
40–41	.00296	94,155	279	94,016	3,406,182	36.18
41–42	.00316	93,876	296	93,728	3,312,166	35.28
42–43	.00336	93,580	314	93,423	3,218,438	34.39
43–44	.00355	93,266	331	93,100	3,125,015	33.51
44–45	.00375	92,935	348	92,761	3,031,915	32.62
45–46	.00399	92,587	370	92,402	2,939,154	31.74
46–47	.00428	92,217	395	92,019	2,846,752	30.87
47–48	.00460	91,822	422	91,611	2,754,733	30.00
48–49	.00494	91,400	452	91,174	2,663,122	29.14
49–50	.00531	90,948	482	90,707	2,571,948	28.28
50–51	.00572	90,466	518	90,206	2,481,241	27.43
51–52	.00623	89,948	561	89,668	2,391,035	26.58
52–53	.00684	89,387	611	89,082	2,301,367	25.75
53–54	.00757	88,776	673	88,439	2,212,285	24.92
54–55	.00840	88,103	740	87,733	2,123,846	24.11

Table 5. Life table for white males: Arizona, 1989–91—Con.

Age in years	Proportion dying	Of 100,000 born alive		Stationary population		Average remaining lifetime
Period of life between two exact ages stated (1)	Proportion of persons alive at beginning of year of age dying during year (2)	Number living at beginning of year of age (3)	Number dying during year of age (4)	In year of age (5)	In this year of age and all subsequent years (6)	Average number of years of life remaining at beginning of year of age (7)
x to $x+1$	q_x	l_x	d_x	L_x	T_x	$\overset{\circ}{e}_x$
55–56	.00931	87,363	813	86,957	2,036,113	23.31
56–57	.01027	86,550	889	86,105	1,949,156	22.52
57–58	.01129	85,661	967	85,177	1,863,051	21.75
58–59	.01236	84,694	1,047	84,170	1,777,874	20.99
59–60	.01346	83,647	1,126	83,084	1,693,704	20.25
60–61	.01458	82,521	1,204	81,919	1,610,620	19.52
61–62	.01575	81,317	1,281	80,677	1,528,701	18.80
62–63	.01703	80,036	1,363	79,355	1,448,024	18.09
63–64	.01843	78,673	1,450	77,948	1,368,669	17.40
64–65	.01991	77,223	1,537	76,455	1,290,721	16.71
65–66	.02135	75,686	1,616	74,878	1,214,266	16.04
66–67	.02280	74,070	1,688	73,226	1,139,388	15.38
67–68	.02447	72,382	1,771	71,496	1,066,162	14.73
68–69	.02652	70,611	1,873	69,674	994,666	14.09
69–70	.02898	68,738	1,992	67,742	924,992	13.46
70–71	.03174	66,746	2,119	65,686	857,250	12.84
71–72	.03467	64,627	2,240	63,507	791,564	12.25
72–73	.03778	62,387	2,357	61,208	728,057	11.67
73–74	.04099	60,030	2,461	58,799	666,849	11.11
74–75	.04434	57,569	2,553	56,293	608,050	10.56
75–76	.04803	55,016	2,642	53,695	551,757	10.03
76–77	.05215	52,374	2,732	51,008	498,062	9.51
77–78	.05659	49,642	2,809	48,237	447,054	9.01
78–79	.06133	46,833	2,872	45,397	398,817	8.52
79–80	.06651	43,961	2,924	42,499	353,420	8.04
80–81	.07260	41,037	2,980	39,547	310,921	7.58
81–82	.07970	38,057	3,033	36,541	271,374	7.13
82–83	.08721	35,024	3,054	33,497	234,833	6.70
83–84	.09458	31,970	3,024	30,457	201,336	6.30
84–85	.10177	28,946	2,946	27,473	170,879	5.90
85–86	.11132	26,000	2,894	24,553	143,406	5.52
86–87	.12284	23,106	2,839	21,687	118,853	5.14
87–88	.13564	20,267	2,749	18,893	97,166	4.79
88–89	.14950	17,518	2,619	16,209	78,273	4.47
89–90	.16431	14,899	2,448	13,675	62,064	4.17
90–91	.18043	12,451	2,246	11,328	48,389	3.89
91–92	.19814	10,205	2,022	9,194	37,061	3.63
92–93	.21644	8,183	1,771	7,297	27,867	3.41
93–94	.23392	6,412	1,500	5,662	20,570	3.21
94–95	.24939	4,912	1,225	4,299	14,908	3.04
95–96	.26329	3,687	971	3,202	10,609	2.88
96–97	.27914	2,716	758	2,337	7,407	2.73
97–98	.29399	1,958	576	1,670	5,070	2.59
98–99	.30869	1,382	426	1,169	3,400	2.46
99–100	.32413	956	310	801	2,231	2.33
100–101	.34033	646	220	536	1,430	2.21
101–102	.35735	426	152	350	894	2.10
102–103	.37522	274	103	222	544	1.99
103–104	.39398	171	67	138	322	1.88
104–105	.41368	104	43	82	184	1.78
105–106	.43436	61	27	48	102	1.68
106–107	.45608	34	15	26	54	1.58
107–108	.47888	19	9	14	28	1.49
108–109	.50282	10	5	8	14	1.41
109–110	.52797	5	3	3	6	1.32

Table 6. Life table for white females ariaona: 1989–91

Age in years	Proportion dying	Of 100,000 born alive		Stationary population		Average remaining lifetime
Period of life between two exact ages stated (1)	Propor ion of persons alive at beginning of year of age dying during year (2)	Number living at beginning of year of age (3)	Number dying during year of age (4)	In year of age (5)	In this year of age and all subsequent years (6)	Average number of years of life remaining at beginning of year of age (7)
x to $x+1$	q_x	l_x	d_x	L_x	T_x	$\overset{\circ}{e}_x$
0–1	.00724	100,000	724	99,421	7,984,498	79.84
1–2	.00067	99,276	66	99,243	7,885,077	79.43
2–3	.00047	99,210	46	99,187	7,785,834	78.48
3–4	.00037	99,164	37	99,145	7,686,647	77.51
4–5	.00028	99,127	28	99,113	7,587,502	76.54
5–6	.00025	99,099	25	99,086	7,488,389	75.56
6–7	.00021	99,074	21	99,064	7,389,303	74.58
7–8	.00018	99,053	18	99,045	7,290,239	73.60
8–9	.00016	99,035	15	99,027	7,191,194	72.61
9–10	.00014	99,020	14	99,013	7,092,167	71.62
10–11	.00013	99,006	13	99,000	6,993,154	70.63
11–12	.00013	98,993	12	98,987	6,894,154	69.64
12–13	.00015	98,981	15	98,973	6,795,167	68.65
13–14	.00020	98,966	20	98,956	6,696,194	67.66
14–15	.00026	98,946	26	98,933	6,597,238	66.68
15–16	.00034	98,920	34	98,903	6,498,305	65.69
16–17	.00041	98,886	40	98,866	6,399,402	64.71
17–18	.00047	98,846	46	98,824	6,300,536	63.74
18–19	.00051	98,800	50	98,775	6,201,712	62.77
19–20	.00054	98,750	53	98,723	6,102,937	61.80
20–21	.00057	98,697	56	98,669	6,004,214	60.83
21–22	.00060	98,641	59	98,612	5,905,545	59.87
22–23	.00061	98,582	60	98,551	5,806,933	58.90
23–24	.00060	98,522	60	98,493	5,708,382	57.94
24–25	.00059	98,462	57	98,433	5,609,889	56.97
25–26	.00057	98,405	56	98,377	5,511,456	56.01
26–27	.00055	98,349	55	98,321	5,413,079	55.04
27–28	.00055	98,294	54	98,267	5,314,758	54.07
28–29	.00056	98,240	55	98,213	5,216,491	53.10
29–30	.00057	98,185	56	98,157	5,118,278	52.13
30–31	.00059	98,129	58	98,101	5,020,121	51.16
31–32	.00061	98,071	60	98,041	4,922,020	50.19
32–33	.00065	98,011	63	97,980	4,823,979	49.22
33–34	.00069	97,948	68	97,913	4,725,999	48.25
34–35	.00075	97,880	74	97,844	4,628,086	47.28
35–36	.00082	97,806	80	97,766	4,530,242	46.32
36–37	.00090	97,726	89	97,681	4,432,476	45.36
37–38	.00098	97,637	96	97,590	4,334,795	44.40
38–39	.00106	97,541	103	97,489	4,237,205	43.44
39–40	.00113	97,438	110	97,383	4,139,716	42.49
40–41	.00121	97,328	118	97,270	4,042,333	41.53
41–42	.00130	97,210	126	97,147	3,945,063	40.58
42–43	.00142	97,084	138	97,015	3,847,916	39.63
43–44	.00158	96,946	153	96,869	3,750,901	38.69
44–45	.00179	96,793	174	96,706	3,654,032	37.75
45–46	.00204	96,619	197	96,521	3,557,326	36.82
46–47	.00231	96,422	223	96,311	3,460,805	35.89
47–48	.00257	96,199	247	96,075	3,364,494	34.97
48–49	.00278	95,952	267	95,818	3,268,419	34.06
49–50	.00297	95,685	284	95,543	3,172,601	33.16
50–51	.00317	95,401	303	95,249	3,077,058	32.25
51–52	.00344	95,098	327	94,935	2,981,809	31.36
52–53	.00375	94,771	355	94,593	2,886,874	30.46
53–54	.00414	94,416	391	94,220	2,792,281	29.57
54–55	.00459	94,025	432	93,809	2,698,061	28.70

Table 6. Life table for white females ariaona: 1989–91—Con.

Age in years	Proportion dying	Of 100,000 born alive		Stationary population		Average remaining lifetime
Period of life between two exact ages stated (1)	Propor ion of persons alive at beginning of year of age dying during year (2)	Number living at beginning of year of age (3)	Number dying during year of age (4)	In year of age (5)	In this year of age and all subsequent years (6)	Average number of years of life remaining at beginning of year of age (7)
x to $x+1$	q_x	l_x	d_x	L_x	T_x	$\overset{\circ}{e}_x$
55–56	.00509	93,593	476	93,355	2,604,252	27.83
56–57	.00562	93,117	524	92,855	2,510,897	26.96
57–58	.00622	92,593	575	92,306	2,418,042	26.11
58–59	.00685	92,018	631	91,702	2,325,736	25.27
59–60	.00752	91,387	687	91,044	2,234,034	24.45
60–61	.00818	90,700	742	90,329	2,142,990	23.63
61–62	.00887	89,958	798	89,559	2,052,661	22.82
62–63	.00960	89,160	855	88,732	1,963,102	22.02
63–64	.01039	88,305	918	87,846	1,874,370	21.23
64–65	.01122	87,387	980	86,897	1,786,524	20.44
65–66	.01204	86,407	1,040	85,888	1,699,627	19.67
66–67	.01288	85,367	1,100	84,817	1,613,739	18.90
67–68	.01382	84,267	1,164	83,685	1,528,922	18.14
68–69	.01496	83,103	1,244	82,480	1,445,237	17.39
69–70	.01633	81,859	1,337	81,191	1,362,757	16.65
70–71	.01791	80,522	1,442	79,802	1,281,566	15.92
71–72	.01965	79,080	1,554	78,303	1,201,764	15.20
72–73	.02160	77,526	1,674	76,689	1,123,461	14.49
73–74	.02370	75,852	1,798	74,953	1,046,772	13.80
74–75	.02593	74,054	1,920	73,094	971,819	13.12
75–76	.02833	72,134	2,044	71,113	898,725	12.46
76–77	.03102	70,090	2,174	69,003	827,612	11.81
77–78	.03408	67,916	2,315	66,759	758,609	11.17
78–79	.03764	65,601	2,469	64,366	691,850	10.55
79–80	.04178	63,132	2,638	61,814	627,484	9.94
80–81	.04658	60,494	2,818	59,085	565,670	9.35
81–82	.05197	57,676	2,997	56,177	506,585	8.78
82–83	.05790	54,679	3,166	53,096	450,408	8.24
83–84	.06425	51,513	3,310	49,858	397,312	7.71
84–85	.07116	48,203	3,430	46,488	347,454	7.21
85–86	.07968	44,773	3,567	42,990	300,966	6.72
86–87	.08970	41,206	3,696	39,358	257,976	6.26
87–88	.10068	37,510	3,777	35,621	218,618	5.83
88–89	.11233	33,733	3,789	31,839	182,997	5.42
89–90	.12473	29,944	3,735	28,077	151,158	5.05
90–91	.13889	26,209	3,640	24,389	123,081	4.70
91–92	.15486	22,569	3,495	20,821	98,692	4.37
92–93	.17113	19,074	3,264	17,442	77,871	4.08
93–94	.18667	15,810	2,951	14,334	60,429	3.82
94–95	.20174	12,859	2,595	11,561	46,095	3.58
95–96	.21737	10,264	2,231	9,149	34,534	3.36
96–97	.23434	8,033	1,882	7,092	25,385	3.16
97–98	.25091	6,151	1,544	5,379	18,293	2.97
98–99	.26715	4,607	1,230	3,992	12,914	2.80
99–100	.28318	3,377	957	2,899	8,922	2.64
100–101	.30017	2,420	726	2,057	6,023	2.49
101–102	.31818	1,694	539	1,424	3,966	2.34
102–103	.33727	1,155	390	961	2,542	2.20
103–104	.35750	765	273	628	1,581	2.07
104–105	.37895	492	187	399	953	1.94
105–106	.40169	305	122	244	554	1.81
106–107	.42579	183	78	144	310	1.70
107–108	.45134	105	47	81	166	1.59
108–109	.47842	58	28	44	85	1.48
109–110	.50712	30	15	22	41	1.38

Table 7. Life table for the population other than white: Arizona, 1989–91

Age in years	Proportion dying	Of 100,000 born alive		Stationary population		Average remaining lifetime
Period of life between two exact ages stated (1)	Proportion of persons alive at beginning of year of age dying during year (2)	Number living at beginning of year of age (3)	Number dying during year of age (4)	In year of age (5)	In this year of age and all subsequent years (6)	Average number of years of life remaining at beginning of year of age (7)
x to $x+1$	q_x	l_x	d_x	L_x	T_x	$\overset{\circ}{e}_x$
0–1	.01314	100,000	1,314	99,021	7,276,474	72.76
1–2	.00125	98,686	123	98,625	7,177,453	72.73
2–3	.00083	98,563	82	98,522	7,078,828	71.82
3–4	.00062	98,481	60	98,451	6,980,306	70.88
4–5	.00050	98,421	50	98,396	6,881,855	69.92
5–6	.00044	98,371	44	98,349	6,783,459	68.96
6–7	.00038	98,327	37	98,308	6,685,110	67.99
7–8	.00034	98,290	33	98,274	6,586,802	67.01
8–9	.00030	98,257	30	98,242	6,488,528	66.04
9–10	.00027	98,227	26	98,214	6,390,286	65.06
10–11	.00025	98,201	24	98,189	6,292,072	64.07
11–12	.00026	98,177	26	98,164	6,193,883	63.09
12–13	.00033	98,151	32	98,135	6,095,719	62.11
13–14	.00047	98,119	46	98,096	5,997,584	61.13
14–15	.00066	98,073	65	98,040	5,899,488	60.15
15–16	.00087	98,008	85	97,966	5,801,448	59.19
16–17	.00107	97,923	104	97,871	5,703,482	58.24
17–18	.00124	97,819	121	97,758	5,605,611	57.31
18–19	.00137	97,698	134	97,631	5,507,853	56.38
19–20	.00146	97,564	142	97,493	5,410,222	55.45
20–21	.00155	97,422	151	97,346	5,312,729	54.53
21–22	.00164	97,271	160	97,191	5,215,383	53.62
22–23	.00172	97,111	167	97,027	5,118,192	52.70
23–24	.00177	96,944	171	96,858	5,021,165	51.79
24–25	.00179	96,773	174	96,686	4,924,307	50.89
25–26	.00181	96,599	175	96,512	4,827,621	49.98
26–27	.00183	96,424	177	96,336	4,731,109	49.07
27–28	.00185	96,247	178	96,158	4,634,773	48.15
28–29	.00187	96,069	179	95,980	4,538,615	47.24
29–30	.00189	95,890	182	95,799	4,442,635	46.33
30–31	.00191	95,708	183	95,617	4,346,836	45.42
31–32	.00194	95,525	186	95,432	4,251,219	44.50
32–33	.00201	95,339	191	95,244	4,155,787	43.59
33–34	.00212	95,148	202	95,047	4,060,543	42.68
34–35	.00228	94,946	216	94,838	3,965,496	41.77
35–36	.00247	94,730	234	94,613	3,870,658	40.86
36–37	.00266	94,496	251	94,370	3,776,045	39.96
37–38	.00286	94,245	270	94,110	3,681,675	39.07
38–39	.00304	93,975	286	93,832	3,587,565	38.18
39–40	.00322	93,689	302	93,538	3,493,733	37.29
40–41	.00340	93,387	317	93,228	3,400,195	36.41
41–42	.00361	93,070	336	92,902	3,306,967	35.53
42–43	.00386	92,734	359	92,555	3,214,065	34.66
43–44	.00417	92,375	385	92,182	3,121,510	33.79
44–45	.00454	91,990	417	91,782	3,029,328	32.93
45–46	.00497	91,573	455	91,345	2,937,546	32.08
46–47	.00544	91,118	496	90,870	2,846,201	31.24
47–48	.00591	90,622	536	90,355	2,755,331	30.40
48–49	.00632	90,086	570	89,801	2,664,976	29.58
49–50	.00668	89,516	598	89,217	2,575,175	28.77
50–51	.00702	88,918	624	88,606	2,485,958	27.96
51–52	.00740	88,294	653	87,968	2,397,352	27.15
52–53	.00789	87,641	691	87,295	2,309,384	26.35
53–54	.00854	86,950	743	86,578	2,222,089	25.56
54–55	.00932	86,207	803	85,806	2,135,511	24.77

Table 7. Life table for the population other than white: Arizona, 1989–91—Con.

Age in years	Proportion dying	Of 100,000 born alive		Stationary population		Average remaining lifetime
Period of life between two exact ages stated (1)	Proportion of persons alive at beginning of year of age dying during year (2)	Number living at beginning of year of age (3)	Number dying during year of age (4)	In year of age (5)	In this year of age and all subsequent years (6)	Average number of years of life remaining at beginning of year of age (7)
x to x+1	q_x	l_x	d_x	L_x	T_x	$\overset{\circ}{e}_x$
55–56	.01018	85,404	870	84,969	2,049,705	24.00
56–57	.01104	84,534	933	84,067	1,964,736	23.24
57–58	.01186	83,601	992	83,105	1,880,669	22.50
58–59	.01262	82,609	1,042	82,088	1,797,564	21.76
59–60	.01337	81,567	1,091	81,022	1,715,476	21.03
60–61	.01412	80,476	1,136	79,907	1,634,454	20.31
61–62	.01499	79,340	1,190	78,745	1,554,547	19.59
62–63	.01611	78,150	1,259	77,521	1,475,802	18.88
63–64	.01755	76,891	1,350	76,216	1,398,281	18.19
64–65	.01924	75,541	1,453	74,814	1,322,065	17.50
65–66	.02109	74,088	1,563	73,307	1,247,251	16.83
66–67	.02295	72,525	1,664	71,693	1,173,944	16.19
67–68	.02479	70,861	1,757	69,982	1,102,251	15.56
68–69	.02659	69,104	1,837	68,186	1,032,269	14.94
69–70	.02847	67,267	1,915	66,309	964,083	14.33
70–71	.03055	65,352	1,997	64,353	897,774	13.74
71–72	.03295	63,355	2,087	62,312	833,421	13.15
72–73	.03572	61,268	2,189	60,173	771,109	12.59
73–74	.03881	59,079	2,293	57,933	710,936	12.03
74–75	.04207	56,786	2,389	55,591	653,003	11.50
75–76	.04538	54,397	2,468	53,163	597,412	10.98
76–77	.04880	51,929	2,535	50,662	544,249	10.48
77–78	.05245	49,394	2,590	48,099	493,587	9.99
78–79	.05656	46,804	2,647	45,481	445,488	9.52
79–80	.06131	44,157	2,708	42,803	400,007	9.06
80–81	.06693	41,449	2,774	40,062	357,204	8.62
81–82	.07313	38,675	2,828	37,261	317,142	8.20
82–83	.07930	35,847	2,842	34,426	279,881	7.81
83–84	.08453	33,005	2,791	31,609	245,455	7.44
84–85	.08865	30,214	2,678	28,876	213,846	7.08
85–86	.09284	27,536	2,556	26,258	184,970	6.72
86–87	.09801	24,980	2,449	23,755	158,712	6.35
87–88	.10450	22,531	2,354	21,354	134,957	5.99
88–89	.11314	20,177	2,283	19,035	113,603	5.63
89–90	.12403	17,894	2,220	16,785	94,568	5.28
90–91	.13701	15,674	2,147	14,600	77,783	4.96
91–92	.15127	13,527	2,046	12,504	63,183	4.67
92–93	.16556	11,481	1,901	10,530	50,679	4.41
93–94	.17713	9,580	1,697	8,732	40,149	4.19
94–95	.18606	7,883	1,467	7,149	31,417	3.99
95–96	.19586	6,416	1,256	5,788	24,268	3.78
96–97	.20830	5,160	1,075	4,623	18,480	3.58
97–98	.22089	4,085	902	3,633	13,857	3.39
98–99	.23370	3,183	744	2,811	10,224	3.21
99–100	.24726	2,439	603	2,137	7,413	3.04
100–101	.26160	1,836	480	1,596	5,276	2.87
101–102	.27677	1,356	376	1,168	3,680	2.71
102–103	.29282	980	287	837	2,512	2.56
103–104	.30981	693	214	586	1,675	2.42
104–105	.32778	479	157	400	1,089	2.28
105–106	.34679	322	112	266	689	2.14
106–107	.36690	210	77	171	423	2.01
107–108	.38818	133	52	107	252	1.89
108–109	.41070	81	33	65	145	1.78
109–110	.43452	48	21	38	80	1.66

Table 8. Life table for males other than white: Arizona, 1989–91

Age in years	Proportion dying	Of 100,000 born alive		Stationary population		Average remaining lifetime
Period of life between two exact ages stated (1)	Proportion of persons alive at beginning of year of age dying during year (2)	Number living at beginning of year of age (3)	Number dying during year of age (4)	In year of age (5)	In this year of age and all subsequent years (6)	Average number of years of life remaining at beginning of year of age (7)
x to x+1	q_x	l_x	d_x	L_x	T_x	$\overset{\circ}{e}_x$
0–1	.01489	100,000	1,489	98,887	6,889,277	68.89
1–2	.00152	98,511	149	98,436	6,790,390	68.93
2–3	.00100	98,362	98	98,313	6,691,954	68.03
3–4	.00071	98,264	70	98,228	6,593,641	67.10
4–5	.00054	98,194	53	98,168	6,495,413	66.15
5–6	.00049	98,141	48	98,116	6,397,245	65.18
6–7	.00043	98,093	42	98,072	6,299,129	64.22
7–8	.00039	98,051	39	98,032	6,201,057	63.24
8–9	.00035	98,012	34	97,995	6,103,025	62.27
9–10	.00031	97,978	30	97,963	6,005,030	61.29
10–11	.00029	97,948	29	97,933	5,907,067	60.31
11–12	.00033	97,919	32	97,903	5,809,134	59.33
12–13	.00045	97,887	44	97,865	5,711,231	58.35
13–14	.00067	97,843	66	97,810	5,613,366	57.37
14–15	.00097	97,777	95	97,729	5,515,556	56.41
15–16	.00131	97,682	128	97,618	5,417,827	55.46
16–17	.00162	97,554	158	97,475	5,320,209	54.54
17–18	.00186	97,396	181	97,306	5,222,734	53.62
18–19	.00202	97,215	197	97,116	5,125,428	52.72
19–20	.00211	97,018	205	96,916	5,028,312	51.83
20–21	.00219	96,813	212	96,707	4,931,396	50.94
21–22	.00227	96,601	219	96,491	4,834,689	50.05
22–23	.00234	96,382	226	96,269	4,738,198	49.16
23–24	.00240	96,156	231	96,041	4,641,929	48.27
24–25	.00245	95,925	235	95,807	4,545,888	47.39
25–26	.00250	95,690	239	95,571	4,450,081	46.51
26–27	.00253	95,451	242	95,330	4,354,510	45.62
27–28	.00257	95,209	244	95,088	4,259,180	44.73
28–29	.00259	94,965	246	94,842	4,164,092	43.85
29–30	.00262	94,719	248	94,595	4,069,250	42.96
30–31	.00264	94,471	249	94,347	3,974,655	42.07
31–32	.00267	94,222	252	94,096	3,880,308	41.18
32–33	.00276	93,970	259	93,840	3,786,212	40.29
33–34	.00294	93,711	276	93,573	3,692,372	39.40
34–35	.00319	93,435	297	93,287	3,598,799	38.52
35–36	.00348	93,138	325	92,975	3,505,512	37.64
36–37	.00379	92,813	352	92,638	3,412,537	36.77
37–38	.00410	92,461	379	92,271	3,319,899	35.91
38–39	.00437	92,082	402	91,881	3,227,628	35.05
39–40	.00461	91,680	422	91,469	3,135,747	34.20
40–41	.00485	91,258	443	91,036	3,044,278	33.36
41–42	.00515	90,815	468	90,581	2,953,242	32.52
42–43	.00549	90,347	496	90,099	2,862,661	31.69
43–44	.00590	89,851	530	89,586	2,772,562	30.86
44–45	.00639	89,321	571	89,036	2,682,976	30.04
45–46	.00697	88,750	618	88,441	2,593,940	29.23
46–47	.00760	88,132	670	87,797	2,505,499	28.43
47–48	.00820	87,462	717	87,104	2,417,702	27.64
48–49	.00870	86,745	754	86,368	2,330,598	26.87
49–50	.00910	85,991	783	85,599	2,244,230	26.10
50–51	.00946	85,208	806	84,805	2,158,631	25.33
51–52	.00987	84,402	833	83,986	2,073,826	24.57
52–53	.01045	83,569	873	83,133	1,989,840	23.81
53–54	.01127	82,696	932	82,230	1,906,707	23.06
54–55	.01231	81,764	1,006	81,261	1,824,477	22.31

Table 8. Life table for males other than white: Arizona, 1989–91—Con.

Age in years	Proportion dying	Of 100,000 born alive		Stationary population		Average remaining lifetime
Period of life between two exact ages stated (1)	Proportion of persons alive at beginning of year of age dying during year (2)	Number living at beginning of year of age (3)	Number dying during year of age (4)	In year of age (5)	In this year of age and all subsequent years (6)	Average number of years of life remaining at beginning of year of age (7)
x to $x+1$	q_x	l_x	d_x	L_x	T_x	$\overset{\circ}{e}_x$
55–56	.01347	80,758	1,088	80,213	1,743,216	21.59
56–57	.01463	79,670	1,166	79,087	1,663,003	20.87
57–58	.01579	78,504	1,239	77,885	1,583,916	20.18
58–59	.01690	77,265	1,306	76,612	1,506,031	19.49
59–60	.01802	75,959	1,369	75,274	1,429,419	18.82
60–61	.01921	74,590	1,432	73,874	1,354,145	18.15
61–62	.02052	73,158	1,502	72,407	1,280,271	17.50
62–63	.02194	71,656	1,572	70,870	1,207,864	16.86
63–64	.02345	70,084	1,644	69,263	1,136,994	16.22
64–65	.02502	68,440	1,712	67,584	1,067,731	15.60
65–66	.02662	66,728	1,776	65,840	1,000,147	14.99
66–67	.02830	64,952	1,838	64,032	934,307	14.38
67–68	.03022	63,114	1,908	62,160	870,275	13.79
68–69	.03254	61,206	1,991	60,211	808,115	13.20
69–70	.03534	59,215	2,093	58,168	747,904	12.63
70–71	.03853	57,122	2,201	56,022	689,736	12.07
71–72	.04203	54,921	2,308	53,766	633,714	11.54
72–73	.04591	52,613	2,416	51,405	579,948	11.02
73–74	.04999	50,197	2,509	48,943	528,543	10.53
74–75	.05416	47,688	2,583	46,396	479,600	10.06
75–76	.05859	45,105	2,643	43,783	433,204	9.60
76–77	.06328	42,462	2,687	41,119	389,421	9.17
77–78	.06786	39,775	2,699	38,425	348,302	8.76
78–79	.07227	37,076	2,680	35,736	309,877	8.36
79–80	.07664	34,396	2,636	33,079	274,141	7.97
80–81	.08122	31,760	2,579	30,471	241,062	7.59
81–82	.08618	29,181	2,515	27,923	210,591	7.22
82–83	.09145	26,666	2,438	25,447	182,668	6.85
83–84	.09701	24,228	2,351	23,052	157,221	6.49
84–85	.10280	21,877	2,249	20,753	134,169	6.13
85–86	.11022	19,628	2,163	18,547	113,416	5.78
86–87	.11839	17,465	2,068	16,431	94,869	5.43
87–88	.12792	15,397	1,969	14,412	78,438	5.09
88–89	.13953	13,428	1,874	12,491	64,026	4.77
89–90	.15353	11,554	1,774	10,667	51,535	4.46
90–91	.17065	9,780	1,669	8,945	40,868	4.18
91–92	.19025	8,111	1,543	7,340	31,923	3.94
92–93	.20909	6,568	1,373	5,881	24,583	3.74
93–94	.22045	5,195	1,145	4,622	18,702	3.60
94–95	.22410	4,050	908	3,596	14,080	3.48
95–96	.22903	3,142	720	2,782	10,484	3.34
96–97	.24048	2,422	582	2,132	7,702	3.18
97–98	.25250	1,840	465	1,607	5,570	3.03
98–99	.26513	1,375	364	1,193	3,963	2.88
99–100	.27838	1,011	282	870	2,770	2.74
100–101	.29230	729	213	623	1,900	2.61
101–102	.30692	516	158	437	1,277	2.47
102–103	.32226	358	116	300	840	2.35
103–104	.33837	242	82	201	540	2.23
104–105	.35529	160	57	132	339	2.11
105–106	.37306	103	38	84	207	2.00
106–107	.39171	65	26	52	123	1.89
107–108	.41130	39	16	32	71	1.79
108–109	.43186	23	10	18	39	1.69
109–110	.45345	13	6	10	21	1.59

Table 9. Life table for females other than white: Arizona, 1989–91

Age in years	Proportion dying	Of 100,000 born alive		Stationary population		Average remaining lifetime
Period of life between two exact ages stated (1)	Proporion of persons alive at beginning of year of age dying during year (2)	Number living at beginning of year of age (3)	Number dying during year of age (4)	In year of age (5)	In this year of age and all subsequent years (6)	Average number of years of life remaining at beginning of year of age (7)
x to $x+1$	q_x	l_x	d_x	L_x	T_x	$\overset{\circ}{e}_x$
0–1	.01135	100,000	1,135	99,158	7,681,422	76.81
1–2	.00098	98,865	97	98,816	7,582,264	76.69
2–3	.00065	98,768	65	98,736	7,483,448	75.77
3–4	.00052	98,703	51	98,677	7,384,712	74.82
4–5	.00047	98,652	47	98,629	7,286,035	73.86
5–6	.00039	98,605	38	98,585	7,187,406	72.89
6–7	.00033	98,567	33	98,550	7,088,821	71.92
7–8	.00029	98,534	28	98,520	6,990,271	70.94
8–9	.00025	98,506	25	98,494	6,891,751	69.96
9–10	.00022	98,481	21	98,470	6,793,257	68.98
10–11	.00020	98,460	20	98,450	6,694,787	68.00
11–12	.00020	98,440	19	98,431	6,596,337	67.01
12–13	.00021	98,421	21	98,410	6,497,906	66.02
13–14	.00026	98,400	26	98,388	6,399,496	65.04
14–15	.00033	98,374	32	98,358	6,301,108	64.05
15–16	.00040	98,342	39	98,322	6,202,750	63.07
16–17	.00048	98,303	48	98,279	6,104,428	62.10
17–18	.00057	98,255	56	98,227	6,006,149	61.13
18–19	.00066	98,199	65	98,166	5,907,922	60.16
19–20	.00075	98,134	73	98,098	5,809,756	59.20
20–21	.00085	98,061	84	98,019	5,711,658	58.25
21–22	.00094	97,977	92	97,931	5,613,639	57.30
22–23	.00102	97,885	100	97,835	5,515,708	56.35
23–24	.00106	97,785	104	97,733	5,417,873	55.41
24–25	.00108	97,681	105	97,628	5,320,140	54.46
25–26	.00108	97,576	106	97,523	5,222,512	53.52
26–27	.00109	97,470	106	97,417	5,124,989	52.58
27–28	.00111	97,364	108	97,310	5,027,572	51.64
28–29	.00113	97,256	110	97,201	4,930,262	50.69
29–30	.00116	97,146	112	97,090	4,833,061	49.75
30–31	.00119	97,034	115	96,976	4,735,971	48.81
31–32	.00122	96,919	118	96,860	4,638,995	47.86
32–33	.00126	96,801	122	96,739	4,542,135	46.92
33–34	.00132	96,679	127	96,616	4,445,396	45.98
34–35	.00139	96,552	134	96,484	4,348,780	45.04
35–36	.00148	96,418	143	96,347	4,252,296	44.10
36–37	.00157	96,275	151	96,199	4,155,949	43.17
37–38	.00168	96,124	161	96,043	4,059,750	42.23
38–39	.00178	95,963	172	95,877	3,963,707	41.30
39–40	.00190	95,791	182	95,701	3,867,830	40.38
40–41	.00202	95,609	193	95,512	3,772,129	39.45
41–42	.00217	95,416	207	95,313	3,676,617	38.53
42–43	.00235	95,209	224	95,096	3,581,304	37.62
43–44	.00256	94,985	244	94,864	3,486,208	36.70
44–45	.00282	94,741	267	94,608	3,391,344	35.80
45–46	.00313	94,474	296	94,326	3,296,736	34.90
46–47	.00348	94,178	328	94,014	3,202,410	34.00
47–48	.00384	93,850	360	93,670	3,108,396	33.12
48–49	.00417	93,490	390	93,296	3,014,726	32.25
49–50	.00449	93,100	418	92,891	2,921,430	31.38
50–51	.00480	92,682	445	92,460	2,828,539	30.52
51–52	.00515	92,237	475	92,000	2,736,079	29.66
52–53	.00557	91,762	511	91,506	2,644,079	28.81
53–54	.00609	91,251	556	90,973	2,552,573	27.97
54–55	.00669	90,695	607	90,392	2,461,600	27.14

Table 9. Life table for females other than white: Arizona, 1989–91—Con.

Age in years	Proportion dying	Of 100,000 born alive		Stationary population		Average remaining lifetime
Period of life between two exact ages stated (1)	Proportion of persons alive at beginning of year of age dying during year (2)	Number living at beginning of year of age (3)	Number dying during year of age (4)	In year of age (5)	In this year of age and all subsequent years (6)	Average number of years of life remaining at beginning of year of age (7)
x to x+1	q_x	l_x	d_x	L_x	T_x	$\overset{\circ}{e}_x$
55–56	.00735	90,088	662	89,758	2,371,208	26.32
56–57	.00801	89,426	716	89,068	2,281,450	25.51
57–58	.00860	88,710	762	88,329	2,192,382	24.71
58–59	.00910	87,948	800	87,548	2,104,053	23.92
59–60	.00957	87,148	834	86,730	2,016,505	23.14
60–61	.00999	86,314	862	85,883	1,929,775	22.36
61–62	.01052	85,452	899	85,003	1,843,892	21.58
62–63	.01141	84,553	964	84,071	1,758,889	20.80
63–64	.01282	83,589	1,072	83,052	1,674,818	20.04
64–65	.01461	82,517	1,206	81,915	1,591,766	19.29
65–66	.01666	81,311	1,354	80,634	1,509,851	18.57
66–67	.01867	79,957	1,494	79,210	1,429,217	17.87
67–68	.02044	78,463	1,603	77,661	1,350,007	17.21
68–69	.02180	76,860	1,676	76,022	1,272,346	16.55
69–70	.02291	75,184	1,722	74,323	1,196,324	15.91
70–71	.02402	73,462	1,765	72,580	1,122,001	15.27
71–72	.02544	71,697	1,824	70,785	1,049,421	14.64
72–73	.02728	69,873	1,906	68,920	978,636	14.01
73–74	.02962	67,967	2,013	66,960	909,716	13.38
74–75	.03231	65,954	2,132	64,888	842,756	12.78
75–76	.03500	63,822	2,233	62,706	777,868	12.19
76–77	.03770	61,589	2,323	60,427	715,162	11.61
77–78	.04081	59,266	2,418	58,057	654,735	11.05
78–79	.04471	56,848	2,542	55,577	596,678	10.50
79–80	.04960	54,306	2,693	52,960	541,101	9.96
80–81	.05578	51,613	2,879	50,173	488,141	9.46
81–82	.06273	48,734	3,057	47,205	437,968	8.99
82–83	.06945	45,677	3,173	44,090	390,763	8.55
83–84	.07443	42,504	3,163	40,923	346,673	8.16
84–85	.07736	39,341	3,044	37,819	305,750	7.77
85–86	.07986	36,297	2,898	34,848	267,931	7.38
86–87	.08364	33,399	2,794	32,002	233,083	6.98
87–88	.08886	30,605	2,719	29,245	201,081	6.57
88–89	.09637	27,886	2,688	26,542	171,836	6.16
89–90	.10626	25,198	2,677	23,860	145,294	5.77
90–91	.11795	22,521	2,657	21,192	121,434	5.39
91–92	.13082	19,864	2,598	18,565	100,242	5.05
92–93	.14466	17,266	2,498	16,017	81,677	4.73
93–94	.15800	14,768	2,333	13,601	65,660	4.45
94–95	.17048	12,435	2,120	11,375	52,059	4.19
95–96	.18338	10,315	1,892	9,369	40,684	3.94
96–97	.19682	8,423	1,658	7,594	31,315	3.72
97–98	.21089	6,765	1,426	6,052	23,721	3.51
98–99	.22557	5,339	1,205	4,737	17,669	3.31
99–100	.23911	4,134	988	3,640	12,932	3.13
100–101	.25346	3,146	798	2,747	9,292	2.95
101–102	.26866	2,348	630	2,033	6,545	2.79
102–103	.28478	1,718	490	1,473	4,512	2.63
103–104	.30187	1,228	370	1,043	3,039	2.47
104–105	.31998	858	275	720	1,996	2.33
105–106	.33918	583	198	484	1,276	2.19
106–107	.35953	385	138	317	792	2.05
107–108	.38110	247	94	199	475	1.93
108–109	.40397	153	62	122	276	1.80
109–110	.42821	91	39	72	154	1.69

Table 10. Life table for the black population: Arizona, 1989–91

Age in years	Proportion dying	Of 100,000 born alive		Stationary population		Average remaining lifetime
Period of life between two exact ages stated (1)	Proportion of persons alive at beginning of year of age dying during year (2)	Number living at beginning of year of age (3)	Number dying during year of age (4)	In year of age (5)	In this year of age and all subsequent years (6)	Average number of years of life remaining at beginning of year of age (7)
x to $x+1$	q_x	l_x	d_x	L_x	T_x	$\overset{\circ}{e}_x$
0–1	.02077	100,000	2,077	98,371	7,084,091	70.84
1–2	.00180	97,923	176	97,835	6,985,720	71.34
2–3	.00123	97,747	120	97,686	6,887,885	70.47
3–4	.00099	97,627	97	97,579	6,790,199	69.55
4–5	.00077	97,530	76	97,492	6,692,620	68.62
5–6	.00064	97,454	62	97,423	6,595,128	67.67
6–7	.00053	97,392	52	97,366	6,497,705	66.72
7–8	.00045	97,340	44	97,318	6,400,339	65.75
8–9	.00039	97,296	38	97,277	6,303,021	64.78
9–10	.00034	97,258	33	97,241	6,205,744	63.81
10–11	.00032	97,225	31	97,210	6,108,503	62.83
11–12	.00034	97,194	33	97,178	6,011,293	61.85
12–13	.00043	97,161	42	97,140	5,914,115	60.87
13–14	.00062	97,119	60	97,089	5,816,975	59.90
14–15	.00086	97,059	83	97,017	5,719,886	58.93
15–16	.00113	96,976	109	96,922	5,622,869	57.98
16–17	.00138	96,867	134	96,800	5,525,947	57.05
17–18	.00158	96,733	153	96,656	5,429,147	56.13
18–19	.00171	96,580	166	96,497	5,332,491	55.21
19–20	.00178	96,414	172	96,329	5,235,994	54.31
20–21	.00184	96,242	177	96,153	5,139,665	53.40
21–22	.00191	96,065	184	95,973	5,043,512	52.50
22–23	.00196	95,881	187	95,788	4,947,539	51.60
23–24	.00199	95,694	190	95,599	4,851,751	50.70
24–25	.00200	95,504	191	95,408	4,756,152	49.80
25–26	.00200	95,313	191	95,218	4,660,744	48.90
26–27	.00201	95,122	191	95,026	4,565,526	48.00
27–28	.00203	94,931	193	94,834	4,470,500	47.09
28–29	.00206	94,738	195	94,641	4,375,666	46.19
29–30	.00210	94,543	199	94,444	4,281,025	45.28
30–31	.00216	94,344	203	94,243	4,186,581	44.38
31–32	.00221	94,141	208	94,036	4,092,338	43.47
32–33	.00229	93,933	216	93,825	3,998,302	42.57
33–34	.00240	93,717	225	93,605	3,904,477	41.66
34–35	.00254	93,492	237	93,373	3,810,872	40.76
35–36	.00270	93,255	253	93,129	3,717,499	39.86
36–37	.00288	93,002	268	92,868	3,624,370	38.97
37–38	.00307	92,734	285	92,592	3,531,502	38.08
38–39	.00328	92,449	303	92,298	3,438,910	37.20
39–40	.00350	92,146	323	91,984	3,346,612	36.32
40–41	.00376	91,823	345	91,651	3,254,628	35.44
41–42	.00404	91,478	370	91,293	3,162,977	34.58
42–43	.00436	91,108	397	90,910	3,071,684	33.71
43–44	.00472	90,711	428	90,496	2,980,774	32.86
44–45	.00511	90,283	462	90,052	2,890,278	32.01
45–46	.00558	89,821	500	89,571	2,800,226	31.18
46–47	.00610	89,321	545	89,049	2,710,655	30.35
47–48	.00659	88,776	586	88,483	2,621,606	29.53
48–49	.00699	88,190	616	87,882	2,533,123	28.72
49–50	.00730	87,574	639	87,254	2,445,241	27.92
50–51	.00756	86,935	657	86,607	2,357,987	27.12
51–52	.00787	86,278	679	85,938	2,271,380	26.33
52–53	.00835	85,599	715	85,241	2,185,442	25.53
53–54	.00905	84,884	768	84,500	2,100,201	24.74
54–55	.00994	84,116	836	83,698	2,015,701	23.96

Table 10. Life table for the black population: Arizona, 1989–91—Con.

Age in years	Proportion dying	Of 100,000 born alive		Stationary population		Average remaining lifetime
Period of life between two exact ages stated (1)	Proportion of persons alive at beginning of year of age dying during year (2)	Number living at beginning of year of age (3)	Number dying during year of age (4)	In year of age (5)	In this year of age and all subsequent years (6)	Average number of years of life remaining at beginning of year of age (7)
x to $x+1$	q_x	l_x	d_x	L_x	T_x	$\overset{\circ}{e}_x$
55–56	.01093	83,280	910	82,825	1,932,003	23.20
56–57	.01190	82,370	980	81,879	1,849,178	22.45
57–58	.01279	81,390	1,041	80,869	1,767,299	21.71
58–59	.01357	80,349	1,091	79,804	1,686,430	20.99
59–60	.01433	79,258	1,136	78,690	1,606,626	20.27
60–61	.01507	78,122	1,177	77,533	1,527,936	19.56
61–62	.01598	76,945	1,230	76,331	1,450,403	18.85
62–63	.01735	75,715	1,313	75,058	1,374,072	18.15
63–64	.01931	74,402	1,437	73,684	1,299,014	17.46
64–65	.02169	72,965	1,583	72,174	1,225,330	16.79
65–66	.02430	71,382	1,735	70,515	1,153,156	16.15
66–67	.02685	69,647	1,870	68,712	1,082,641	15.54
67–68	.02916	67,777	1,976	66,789	1,013,929	14.96
68–69	.03111	65,801	2,047	64,778	947,140	14.39
69–70	.03284	63,754	2,094	62,707	882,362	13.84
70–71	.03454	61,660	2,130	60,595	819,655	13.29
71–72	.03647	59,530	2,171	58,445	759,060	12.75
72–73	.03878	57,359	2,224	56,247	700,615	12.21
73–74	.04167	55,135	2,297	53,986	644,368	11.69
74–75	.04507	52,838	2,382	51,647	590,382	11.17
75–76	.04883	50,456	2,463	49,225	538,735	10.68
76–77	.05277	47,993	2,533	46,726	489,510	10.20
77–78	.05688	45,460	2,586	44,167	442,784	9.74
78–79	.06105	42,874	2,617	41,566	398,617	9.30
79–80	.06535	40,257	2,631	38,942	357,051	8.87
80–81	.07011	37,626	2,638	36,307	318,109	8.45
81–82	.07541	34,988	2,638	33,669	281,802	8.05
82–83	.08088	32,350	2,617	31,041	248,133	7.67
83–84	.08627	29,733	2,565	28,451	217,092	7.30
84–85	.09155	27,168	2,487	25,925	188,641	6.94
85–86	.09751	24,681	2,407	23,477	162,716	6.59
86–87	.10418	22,274	2,320	21,114	139,239	6.25
87–88	.11137	19,954	2,223	18,842	118,125	5.92
88–89	.11933	17,731	2,115	16,674	99,283	5.60
89–90	.12832	15,616	2,004	14,614	82,609	5.29
90–91	.13853	13,612	1,886	12,669	67,995	5.00
91–92	.15008	11,726	1,760	10,846	55,326	4.72
92–93	.16261	9,966	1,620	9,156	44,480	4.46
93–94	.17475	8,346	1,459	7,617	35,324	4.23
94–95	.18514	6,887	1,275	6,249	27,707	4.02
95–96	.19386	5,612	1,088	5,069	21,458	3.82
96–97	.20590	4,524	931	4,058	16,389	3.62
97–98	.21821	3,593	784	3,201	12,331	3.43
98–99	.23087	2,809	649	2,484	9,130	3.25
99–100	.24426	2,160	527	1,897	6,646	3.08
100–101	.25843	1,633	422	1,421	4,749	2.91
101–102	.27342	1,211	331	1,046	3,328	2.75
102–103	.28927	880	255	752	2,282	2.59
103–104	.30605	625	191	530	1,530	2.45
104–105	.32380	434	141	363	1,000	2.31
105–106	.34258	293	100	243	637	2.17
106–107	.36245	193	70	158	394	2.04
107–108	.38348	123	47	100	236	1.92
108–109	.40572	76	31	60	136	1.80
109–110	.42925	45	19	35	76	1.69

Table 11. Life table for black males: Arizona, 1989–91

Age in years	Proportion dying	Of 100,000 born alive		Stationary population		Average remaining lifetime
Period of life between two exact ages stated (1)	Proportion of persons alive at beginning of year of age dying during year (2)	Number living at beginning of year of age (3)	Number dying during year of age (4)	In year of age (5)	In this year of age and all subsequent years (6)	Average number of years of life remaining at beginning of year of age (7)
x to $x+1$	q_x	l_x	d_x	L_x	T_x	$\overset{\circ}{e}_x$
0–1	.02369	100,000	2,369	98,076	6,720,240	67.20
1–2	.00207	97,631	202	97,530	6,622,164	67.83
2–3	.00137	97,429	134	97,362	6,524,634	66.97
3–4	.00107	97,295	104	97,243	6,427,272	66.06
4–5	.00082	97,191	80	97,151	6,330,029	65.13
5–6	.00071	97,111	69	97,077	6,232,878	64.18
6–7	.00062	97,042	59	97,013	6,135,801	63.23
7–8	.00055	96,983	53	96,956	6,038,788	62.27
8–9	.00048	96,930	47	96,906	5,941,832	61.30
9–10	.00043	96,883	42	96,862	5,844,926	60.33
10–11	.00040	96,841	38	96,823	5,748,064	59.36
11–12	.00043	96,803	42	96,782	5,651,241	58.38
12–13	.00058	96,761	56	96,732	5,554,459	57.40
13–14	.00086	96,705	84	96,663	5,457,727	56.44
14–15	.00123	96,621	119	96,562	5,361,064	55.49
15–16	.00163	96,502	157	96,423	5,264,502	54.55
16–17	.00199	96,345	192	96,249	5,168,079	53.64
17–18	.00226	96,153	217	96,045	5,071,830	52.75
18–19	.00240	95,936	230	95,821	4,975,785	51.87
19–20	.00244	95,706	234	95,590	4,879,964	50.99
20–21	.00247	95,472	235	95,354	4,784,374	50.11
21–22	.00250	95,237	238	95,118	4,689,020	49.24
22–23	.00253	94,999	241	94,879	4,593,902	48.36
23–24	.00256	94,758	242	94,637	4,499,023	47.48
24–25	.00259	94,516	244	94,394	4,404,386	46.60
25–26	.00261	94,272	246	94,149	4,309,992	45.72
26–27	.00262	94,026	247	93,902	4,215,843	44.84
27–28	.00265	93,779	248	93,655	4,121,941	43.95
28–29	.00269	93,531	252	93,405	4,028,286	43.07
29–30	.00274	93,279	255	93,152	3,934,881	42.18
30–31	.00279	93,024	259	92,895	3,841,729	41.30
31–32	.00286	92,765	265	92,632	3,748,834	40.41
32–33	.00296	92,500	274	92,362	3,656,202	39.53
33–34	.00312	92,226	288	92,082	3,563,840	38.64
34–35	.00333	91,938	306	91,785	3,471,758	37.76
35–36	.00357	91,632	327	91,469	3,379,973	36.89
36–37	.00383	91,305	349	91,131	3,288,504	36.02
37–38	.00411	90,956	374	90,769	3,197,373	35.15
38–39	.00440	90,582	398	90,383	3,106,604	34.30
39–40	.00471	90,184	425	89,971	3,016,221	33.45
40–41	.00505	89,759	453	89,533	2,926,250	32.60
41–42	.00544	89,306	486	89,063	2,836,717	31.76
42–43	.00586	88,820	520	88,560	2,747,654	30.94
43–44	.00630	88,300	557	88,021	2,659,094	30.11
44–45	.00678	87,743	595	87,446	2,571,073	29.30
45–46	.00735	87,148	640	86,828	2,483,627	28.50
46–47	.00799	86,508	691	86,162	2,396,799	27.71
47–48	.00860	85,817	738	85,448	2,310,637	26.93
48–49	.00910	85,079	774	84,692	2,225,189	26.15
49–50	.00949	84,305	801	83,904	2,140,497	25.39
50–51	.00981	83,504	819	83,095	2,056,593	24.63
51–52	.01020	82,685	843	82,264	1,973,498	23.87
52–53	.01082	81,842	885	81,400	1,891,234	23.11
53–54	.01179	80,957	955	80,479	1,809,834	22.36
54–55	.01303	80,002	1,042	79,481	1,729,355	21.62

Table 11. Life table for black males: Arizona, 1989–91—Con.

Age in years	Proportion dying	Of 100,000 born alive		Stationary population		Average remaining lifetime
Period of life between two exact ages stated (1)	Proportion of persons alive at beginning of year of age dying during year (2)	Number living at beginning of year of age (3)	Number dying during year of age (4)	In year of age (5)	In this year of age and all subsequent years (6)	Average number of years of life remaining at beginning of year of age (7)
x to $x+1$	q_x	l_x	d_x	L_x	T_x	$\overset{\circ}{e}_x$
55–56	.01440	78,960	1,137	78,391	1,649,874	20.90
56–57	.01570	77,823	1,222	77,212	1,571,483	20.19
57–58	.01686	76,601	1,291	75,956	1,494,271	19.51
58–59	.01785	75,310	1,344	74,638	1,418,315	18.83
59–60	.01878	73,966	1,389	73,271	1,343,677	18.17
60–61	.01970	72,577	1,430	71,861	1,270,406	17.50
61–62	.02085	71,147	1,484	70,405	1,198,545	16.85
62–63	.02248	69,663	1,566	68,880	1,128,140	16.19
63–64	.02473	68,097	1,684	67,255	1,059,260	15.56
64–65	.02741	66,413	1,820	65,503	992,005	14.94
65–66	.03031	64,593	1,958	63,614	926,502	14.34
66–67	.03318	62,635	2,078	61,596	862,888	13.78
67–68	.03590	60,557	2,174	59,470	801,292	13.23
68–69	.03839	58,383	2,241	57,263	741,822	12.71
69–70	.04076	56,142	2,289	54,997	684,559	12.19
70–71	.04309	53,853	2,320	52,693	629,562	11.69
71–72	.04562	51,533	2,351	50,357	576,869	11.19
72–73	.04868	49,182	2,395	47,985	526,512	10.71
73–74	.05259	46,787	2,460	45,557	478,527	10.23
74–75	.05738	44,327	2,544	43,055	432,970	9.77
75–76	.06306	41,783	2,634	40,466	389,915	9.33
76–77	.06917	39,149	2,708	37,794	349,449	8.93
77–78	.07507	36,441	2,736	35,073	311,655	8.55
78–79	.07993	33,705	2,694	32,358	276,582	8.21
79–80	.08369	31,011	2,595	29,714	244,224	7.88
80–81	.08716	28,416	2,477	27,177	214,510	7.55
81–82	.09109	25,939	2,363	24,758	187,333	7.22
82–83	.09502	23,576	2,240	22,456	162,575	6.90
83–84	.09912	21,336	2,115	20,278	140,119	6.57
84–85	.10336	19,221	1,987	18,228	119,841	6.23
85–86	.10935	17,234	1,884	16,293	101,613	5.90
86–87	.11581	15,350	1,778	14,461	85,320	5.56
87–88	.12372	13,572	1,679	12,732	70,859	5.22
88–89	.13388	11,893	1,592	11,097	58,127	4.89
89–90	.14666	10,301	1,511	9,546	47,030	4.57
90–91	.16262	8,790	1,429	8,075	37,484	4.26
91–92	.18212	7,361	1,341	6,691	29,409	4.00
92–93	.20454	6,020	1,231	5,404	22,718	3.77
93–94	.22139	4,789	1,060	4,259	17,314	3.62
94–95	.22482	3,729	839	3,309	13,055	3.50
95–96	.22659	2,890	655	2,563	9,746	3.37
96–97	.23792	2,235	531	1,969	7,183	3.21
97–98	.24982	1,704	426	1,491	5,214	3.06
98–99	.26231	1,278	335	1,111	3,723	2.91
99–100	.27542	943	260	813	2,612	2.77
100–101	.28920	683	197	584	1,799	2.63
101–102	.30365	486	148	412	1,215	2.50
102–103	.31884	338	108	284	803	2.38
103–104	.33478	230	77	192	519	2.25
104–105	.35152	153	54	126	327	2.14
105–106	.36909	99	36	81	201	2.02
106–107	.38755	63	25	50	120	1.92
107–108	.40693	38	15	31	70	1.81
108–109	.42727	23	10	18	39	1.71
109–110	.44864	13	6	10	21	1.61

Table 12. Life table for black females: Arizona, 1989–91

Age in years	Proportion dying	Of 100,000 born alive		Stationary population		Average remaining lifetime
Period of life between two exact ages stated (1)	Proportion of persons alive at beginning of year of age dying during year (2)	Number living at beginning of year of age (3)	Number dying during year of age (4)	In year of age (5)	In this year of age and all subsequent years (6)	Average number of years of life remaining at beginning of year of age (7)
x to $x+1$	q_x	l_x	d_x	L_x	T_x	$\overset{\circ}{e}_x$
0–1	.01776	100,000	1,776	98,672	7,489,738	74.90
1–2	.00153	98,224	150	98,149	7,391,066	75.25
2–3	.00108	98,074	106	98,021	7,292,917	74.36
3–4	.00092	97,968	90	97,922	7,194,896	73.44
4–5	.00072	97,878	70	97,843	7,096,974	72.51
5–6	.00057	97,808	56	97,780	6,999,131	71.56
6–7	.00045	97,752	44	97,730	6,901,351	70.60
7–8	.00036	97,708	35	97,691	6,803,621	69.63
8–9	.00029	97,673	29	97,659	6,705,930	68.66
9–10	.00025	97,644	24	97,632	6,608,271	67.68
10–11	.00023	97,620	23	97,609	6,510,639	66.69
11–12	.00024	97,597	23	97,585	6,413,030	65.71
12–13	.00028	97,574	27	97,561	6,315,445	64.72
13–14	.00035	97,547	34	97,529	6,217,884	63.74
14–15	.00045	97,513	44	97,491	6,120,355	62.76
15–16	.00057	97,469	55	97,441	6,022,864	61.79
16–17	.00069	97,414	67	97,380	5,925,423	60.83
17–18	.00080	97,347	79	97,308	5,828,043	59.87
18–19	.00090	97,268	87	97,224	5,730,735	58.92
19–20	.00099	97,181	97	97,133	5,633,511	57.97
20–21	.00108	97,084	105	97,031	5,536,378	57.03
21–22	.00117	96,979	113	96,923	5,439,347	56.09
22–23	.00124	96,866	120	96,805	5,342,424	55.15
23–24	.00127	96,746	123	96,684	5,245,619	54.22
24–25	.00128	96,623	124	96,561	5,148,935	53.29
25–26	.00127	96,499	123	96,438	5,052,374	52.36
26–27	.00128	96,376	123	96,315	4,955,936	51.42
27–28	.00129	96,253	124	96,191	4,859,621	50.49
28–29	.00132	96,129	126	96,066	4,763,430	49.55
29–30	.00136	96,003	131	95,938	4,667,364	48.62
30–31	.00140	95,872	134	95,805	4,571,426	47.68
31–32	.00145	95,738	139	95,668	4,475,621	46.75
32–33	.00150	95,599	144	95,528	4,379,953	45.82
33–34	.00156	95,455	148	95,381	4,284,425	44.88
34–35	.00162	95,307	155	95,229	4,189,044	43.95
35–36	.00170	95,152	162	95,071	4,093,815	43.02
36–37	.00179	94,990	170	94,905	3,998,744	42.10
37–38	.00188	94,820	178	94,731	3,903,839	41.17
38–39	.00199	94,642	189	94,547	3,809,108	40.25
39–40	.00212	94,453	200	94,353	3,714,561	39.33
40–41	.00226	94,253	213	94,146	3,620,208	38.41
41–42	.00243	94,040	229	93,926	3,526,062	37.50
42–43	.00264	93,811	247	93,687	3,432,136	36.59
43–44	.00290	93,564	271	93,429	3,338,449	35.68
44–45	.00321	93,293	300	93,143	3,245,020	34.78
45–46	.00359	92,993	334	92,826	3,151,877	33.89
46–47	.00401	92,659	371	92,474	3,059,051	33.01
47–48	.00441	92,288	407	92,084	2,966,577	32.14
48–49	.00472	91,881	434	91,664	2,874,493	31.28
49–50	.00496	91,447	454	91,220	2,782,829	30.43
50–51	.00519	90,993	472	90,757	2,691,609	29.58
51–52	.00546	90,521	495	90,274	2,600,852	28.73
52–53	.00580	90,026	522	89,765	2,510,578	27.89
53–54	.00625	89,504	560	89,224	2,420,813	27.05
54–55	.00679	88,944	604	88,643	2,331,589	26.21

Table 12. Life table for black females: Arizona, 1989–91—Con.

Age in years	Proportion dying	Of 100,000 born alive		Stationary population		Average remaining lifetime
Period of life between two exact ages stated (1)	Proportion of persons alive at beginning of year of age dying during year (2)	Number living at beginning of year of age (3)	Number dying during year of age (4)	In year of age (5)	In this year of age and all subsequent years (6)	Average number of years of life remaining at beginning of year of age (7)
x to $x+1$	q_x	l_x	d_x	L_x	T_x	$\overset{\circ}{e}_x$
55–56	.00740	88,340	654	88,013	2,242,946	25.39
56–57	.00804	87,686	705	87,333	2,154,933	24.58
57–58	.00869	86,981	755	86,604	2,067,600	23.77
58–59	.00935	86,226	806	85,823	1,980,996	22.97
59–60	.01007	85,420	861	84,989	1,895,173	22.19
60–61	.01077	84,559	911	84,104	1,810,184	21.41
61–62	.01161	83,648	971	83,162	1,726,080	20.63
62–63	.01287	82,677	1,065	82,145	1,642,918	19.87
63–64	.01468	81,612	1,198	81,013	1,560,773	19.12
64–65	.01687	80,414	1,357	79,736	1,479,760	18.40
65–66	.01929	79,057	1,525	78,294	1,400,024	17.71
66–67	.02163	77,532	1,677	76,694	1,321,730	17.05
67–68	.02364	75,855	1,793	74,958	1,245,036	16.41
68–69	.02517	74,062	1,864	73,130	1,170,078	15.80
69–70	.02639	72,198	1,905	71,245	1,096,948	15.19
70–71	.02755	70,293	1,937	69,325	1,025,703	14.59
71–72	.02897	68,356	1,980	67,365	956,378	13.99
72–73	.03073	66,376	2,040	65,356	889,013	13.39
73–74	.03298	64,336	2,122	63,275	823,657	12.80
74–75	.03565	62,214	2,218	61,105	760,382	12.22
75–76	.03846	59,996	2,307	58,842	699,277	11.66
76–77	.04137	57,689	2,387	56,496	640,435	11.10
77–78	.04471	55,302	2,472	54,066	583,939	10.56
78–79	.04868	52,830	2,572	51,544	529,873	10.03
79–80	.05340	50,258	2,684	48,916	478,329	9.52
80–81	.05898	47,574	2,806	46,171	429,413	9.03
81–82	.06519	44,768	2,918	43,309	383,242	8.56
82–83	.07167	41,850	3,000	40,350	339,933	8.12
83–84	.07789	38,850	3,026	37,337	299,583	7.71
84–85	.08386	35,824	3,004	34,322	262,246	7.32
85–86	.09020	32,820	2,960	31,340	227,924	6.94
86–87	.09754	29,860	2,913	28,403	196,584	6.58
87–88	.10499	26,947	2,829	25,533	168,181	6.24
88–89	.11237	24,118	2,710	22,762	142,648	5.91
89–90	.11996	21,408	2,569	20,124	119,886	5.60
90–91	.12808	18,839	2,413	17,633	99,762	5.30
91–92	.13734	16,426	2,256	15,298	82,129	5.00
92–93	.14797	14,170	2,096	13,122	66,831	4.72
93–94	.15981	12,074	1,930	11,109	53,709	4.45
94–95	.17174	10,144	1,742	9,273	42,600	4.20
95–96	.18244	8,402	1,533	7,636	33,327	3.97
96–97	.19556	6,869	1,343	6,197	25,691	3.74
97–98	.20946	5,526	1,158	4,947	19,494	3.53
98–99	.22414	4,368	979	3,879	14,547	3.33
99–100	.23758	3,389	805	2,987	10,668	3.15
100–101	.25184	2,584	651	2,258	7,681	2.97
101–102	.26695	1,933	516	1,676	5,423	2.80
102–103	.28297	1,417	401	1,216	3,747	2.64
103–104	.29994	1,016	305	864	2,531	2.49
104–105	.31794	711	226	598	1,667	2.34
105–106	.33702	485	163	404	1,069	2.20
106–107	.35724	322	115	264	665	2.07
107–108	.37867	207	79	168	401	1.94
108–109	.40139	128	51	102	233	1.82
109–110	.42548	77	33	61	131	1.70

Table 13. Standard errors of the probability of dying: Arizona, 1989–91

Exact age in years	Total Both sexes	Total Male	Total Female	White Both sexes	White Male	White Female	All o her Total Both sexes	All o her Total Male	All o her Total Female	All o her Black Both sexes	All o her Black Male	All o her Black Female
0	.000208	.000307	.000280	.000216	.000317	.000291	.000665	000996	.000878	.001636	.002450	.002157
1	.000065	.000096	.000086	.000067	.000098	.000090	.000208	000323	.000262	.000499	.000755	.000652
2	.000058	.000088	.000076	.000061	.000092	.000080	.000172	000266	.000218	.000403	.000595	.000540
3	.000051	.000076	.000068	.000054	.000079	.000072	.000151	000227	.000197	.000367	.000532	.000505
4	.000046	.000069	.000060	.000048	.000073	.000062	.000138	000199	.000190	.000328	.000473	.000452
5	.000043	.000063	.000056	.000044	.000066	.000059	.000131	000193	.000175	.000302	.000446	.000405
6	.000040	.000060	.000052	.000041	.000062	.000054	.000123	000183	.000163	.000279	.000420	.000364
7	.000037	.000056	.000049	.000039	.000059	.000051	.000117	000176	.000153	.000260	.000400	.000330
8	.000035	.000053	.000046	.000036	.000054	.000048	.000111	000169	.000144	.000244	.000381	.000294
9	.000032	.000048	.000044	.000033	.000049	.000045	.000106	000162	.000137	.000231	.000364	.000251
10	.000030	.000044	.000042	.000031	.000044	.000044	.000104	000160	.000132	.000226	.000356	.000231
11	.000031	.000045	.000043	.000032	.000045	.000045	.000108	000170	.000133	.000236	.000375	.000239
12	.000037	.000056	.000046	.000038	.000057	.000049	.000123	000201	.000141	.000270	.000437	.000279
13	.000046	.000074	.000053	.000048	.000076	.000056	.000147	000247	.000156	.000322	.000531	.000350
14	.000056	.000093	.000060	.000059	.000096	.000064	.000174	000297	.000175	.000379	.000629	.000397
15	.000065	.000109	.000068	.000068	.000114	.000072	.000199	000342	.000195	.000433	.000717	.000446
16	.000072	.000122	.000074	.000076	.000128	.000079	.000221	000379	.000214	.000477	.000785	.000493
17	.000078	.000131	.000079	.000082	.000137	.000084	.000238	000406	.000232	.000509	.000829	.000533
18	.000081	.000136	.000083	.000085	.000143	.000087	.000251	000424	.000251	.000528	.000849	.000567
19	.000083	.000139	.000085	.000087	.000146	.000089	.000261	000434	.000270	.000539	.000853	.000596
20	.000085	.000142	.000088	.000089	.000149	.000091	.000270	000443	.000290	.000548	.000854	.000627
21	.000086	.000144	.000090	.000090	.000151	.000093	.000280	000452	.000308	.000557	.000856	.000654
22	.000087	.000144	.000091	.000090	.000151	.000093	.000286	000459	.000320	.000560	.000854	.000669
23	.000086	.000143	.000089	.000089	.000149	.000091	.000287	000462	.000324	.000557	.000848	.000668
24	.000084	.000140	.000087	.000087	.000146	.000088	.000286	000464	.000321	.000549	.000840	.000656
25	.000081	.000137	.000084	.000084	.000142	.000085	.000284	000464	.000316	.000540	.000832	.000641
26	.000080	.000135	.000082	.000082	.000139	.000083	.000283	000465	.000313	.000533	.000825	.000630
27	.000079	.000134	.000081	.000081	.000138	.000081	.000283	000467	.000313	.000531	.000824	.000626
28	.000079	.000135	.000081	.000082	.000140	.000081	.000286	000472	.000316	.000535	.000830	.000632
29	.000081	.000138	.000082	.000083	.000143	.000082	.000290	000480	.000322	.000544	.000843	.000646
30	.000082	.000141	.000083	.000085	.000147	.000083	.000295	000488	.000329	.000555	.000857	.000662
31	.000084	.000145	.000084	.000087	.000150	.000085	.000301	000499	.000337	.000567	.000875	.000679
32	.000086	.000148	.000087	.000089	.000154	.000088	.000310	000515	.000347	.000584	.000902	.000699
33	.000089	.000153	.000090	.000092	.000158	.000091	.000324	000542	.000360	.000607	.000940	.000722
34	.000092	.000157	.000095	.000095	.000162	.000096	.000343	000576	.000377	.000635	.000989	.000749
35	.000096	.000163	.000100	.000098	.000167	.000102	.000364	000616	.000396	.000668	.001046	.000780
36	.000100	.000169	.000106	.000102	.000173	.000108	.000388	000660	.000418	.000705	.001110	.000816
37	.000104	.000176	.000112	.000106	.000179	.000114	.000412	000703	.000441	.000747	.001179	.000858
38	.000109	.000183	.000117	.000111	.000186	.000120	.000435	000744	.000465	.000792	.001253	.000906
39	.000113	.000191	.000123	.000116	.000194	.000125	.000457	000784	.000491	.000842	.001333	.000961
40	.000118	.000199	.000128	.000121	.000203	.000130	.000481	000825	.000518	.000899	.001423	.001025
41	.000124	.000208	.000134	.000126	.000212	.000137	.000509	000873	.000550	.000964	.001525	.001098
42	.000130	.000218	.000142	.000133	.000222	.000145	.000541	000928	.000587	.001036	.001638	.001183
43	.000138	.000229	.000153	.000140	.000233	.000156	.000580	000994	.000632	.001117	.001764	.001284
44	.000147	.000243	.000166	.000150	.000247	.000170	.000626	001071	.000685	.001206	.001903	.001399
45	.000158	.000259	.000182	.000160	.000262	.000186	.000679	001161	.000747	.001310	.002067	.001533
46	.000170	.000277	.000199	.000172	.000280	.000203	.000737	001258	.000815	.001426	.002250	.001679
47	.000182	.000296	.000215	.000185	.000299	.000220	.000793	001351	.000883	.001536	.002427	.001817
48	.000193	.000314	.000228	.000196	.000318	.000234	.000841	001428	.000944	.001626	.002575	.001928
49	.000203	.000332	.000241	.000207	.000337	.000246	.000881	001488	.000998	.001697	.002693	.002013
50	.000215	.000351	.000253	.000219	.000357	.000259	.000917	001541	.001049	.001758	.002795	.002089
51	.000228	.000373	.000268	.000232	.000380	.000275	.000958	001601	.001105	.001827	.002910	.002175
52	.000242	.000396	.000284	.000247	.000405	.000291	.001005	001675	.001167	.001909	.003050	.002270
53	.000257	.000421	.000302	.000263	.000431	.000309	.001062	001772	.001236	.002013	.003228	.002382
54	.000272	.000447	.000320	.000279	.000458	.000328	.001127	001890	.001310	.002133	.003433	.002509
55	.000288	.000473	.000339	.000295	.000484	.000347	.001194	002016	.001386	.002255	.003637	.002641
56	.000303	.000498	.000357	.000311	.000510	.000366	.001260	002139	.001460	.002369	.003826	.002770
57	.000318	.000523	.000374	.000326	.000535	.000384	.001326	002266	.001531	.002483	.004017	.002905
58	.000331	.000546	.000390	.000340	.000559	.000400	.001395	002397	.001602	.002602	.004224	.003051
59	.000343	.000568	.000403	.000352	.000581	.000415	.001468	002535	.001678	.002733	.004461	.003213

Table 13. Standard errors of the probability of dying: Arizona, 1989–91—Con.

| Exact age in years | Total | | | White | | | All other | | | | | |
| | | | | | | | Total | | | Black | | |
	Both sexes	Male	Female	Both sexes	Male	Female	Both sexes	Male	Female	Both sexes	Male	Female
60	.000354	.000589	.000416	.000363	.000602	.000428	.001546	002685	.001755	.002870	.004722	.003376
61	.000365	.000610	.000428	.000374	.000623	.000440	.001632	002846	.001842	.003024	.005012	.003558
62	.000376	.000631	.000441	.000385	.000644	.000452	.001729	003011	.001960	.003212	.005346	.003794
63	.000387	.000651	.000454	.000396	.000664	.000464	.001838	003173	.002114	.003435	.005713	.004088
64	.000399	.000671	.000467	.000407	.000684	.000476	.001954	003331	.002291	.003675	.006089	.004412
65	.000409	.000689	.000479	.000416	.000702	.000487	.002074	003485	.002479	.003920	.006469	.004744
66	.000419	.000707	.000492	.000427	.000720	.000499	.002199	003652	.002666	.004161	.006856	.005060
67	.000435	.000734	.000510	.000442	.000747	.000516	.002334	003853	.002851	.004396	.007243	.005353
68	.000457	.000773	.000536	.000464	.000786	.000543	.002490	004113	.003037	.004628	.007642	.005627
69	.000487	.000823	.000570	.000495	.000837	.000578	.002674	004438	.003236	.004872	.008068	.005903
70	.000522	.000881	.000612	.000530	.000896	.000620	.002889	004818	.003466	.005132	.008509	.006201
71	.000560	.000944	.000657	.000569	.000959	.000667	.003132	005234	.003733	.005417	.008985	.006538
72	.000601	.001012	.000706	.000610	.001028	.000717	.003390	005678	.004024	.005746	.009561	.006917
73	.000643	.001085	.000757	.000653	.001101	.000768	.003644	006122	.004318	.006129	.010290	.007338
74	.000686	.001162	.000808	.000697	.001180	.000820	.003885	006557	.004599	.006566	.011181	.007796
75	.000734	.001250	.000864	.000746	.001269	.000877	.004122	007013	.004863	.007051	.012247	.008273
76	.000789	.001351	.000928	.000802	.001373	.000943	.004381	007514	.005148	.007582	.013436	.008794
77	.000852	.001467	.001002	.000866	.001491	.001018	.004681	008051	.005503	.008165	.014676	.009412
78	.000926	.001599	.001091	.000941	.001626	.001108	.005059	008648	.005995	.008805	.015856	.010180
79	.001013	.001753	.001196	.001030	.001784	.001216	.005534	009324	.006652	.009514	.016972	.011124
80	.001116	.001939	.001321	.001135	.001975	.001341	.006112	010090	.007490	.010331	.018162	.012254
81	.001236	.002162	.001463	.001257	.002205	.001485	.006763	010946	.008444	.011267	.019547	.013537
82	.001373	.002418	.001625	.001397	.002469	.001649	.007454	011889	.009435	.012298	.021053	.014953
83	.001525	.002700	.001806	.001553	.002761	.001834	.008111	012900	.010295	.013403	.022704	.016445
84	.001696	.003013	.002011	.001728	.003086	.002045	.008721	013988	.010991	.014597	.024529	.018031
85	.001906	.003410	.002262	.001946	.003499	.002306	.009356	015244	.011662	.015963	.026655	.019846
86	.002165	.003913	.002568	.002217	.004025	.002624	.010124	016701	.012524	.017569	.029080	.022032
87	.002474	.004522	.002927	.002537	.004663	.002996	.011113	018540	.013664	.019499	.032247	.024529
88	.002836	.005252	.003344	.002912	.005425	.003426	.012506	021050	.015319	.021930	.036781	.027389
89	.003265	.006133	.003835	.003352	.006336	.003929	.014454	024535	.017655	.025065	.043403	.030737
90	.003808	.007262	.004451	.003905	.007494	.004557	.017194	029631	.020854	.029284	.053729	.034825
91	.004508	.008770	.005238	.004620	.009035	.005360	.020879	036951	.024992	.034932	.070176	.039932
92	.005364	.010697	.006182	.005493	.011002	.006323	.025473	046590	.030055	.042038	.095683	.046141
93	.006343	.012993	.007247	.006498	.013376	.007415	.029932	055844	.035136	.049670	.123986	.053370
94	.007414	.015523	.008418	.007615	.016062	.008628	.033198	061214	.039379	.056656	.136955	.061479
95	.007892	.016610	.009085	.008111	.017196	.009313	.035593	066385	.043898	.056778	.115867	.065581
96	.009378	.019828	.010788	.009650	.020616	.011064	.041478	075795	.051767	.066408	.131950	.077846
97	.011262	.023985	.012941	.011606	.025039	.013284	.048973	089264	.061524	.077775	.155511	.091486
98	.013741	.029722	.015770	.014211	.031052	.016248	.057757	.109716	.071941	.091237	.190381	.106427
99	.016686	.036846	.019037	.017315	.038799	.019659	.067552	.126616	.084475	.106592	.219396	.124828
100	.020684	.046159	.023533	.021591	.048981	.024438	.078986	.149363	.098403	.125886	.265023	.146224
101	.026138	.058630	.029700	.027455	.062638	.031035	.094552	.181089	.117236	.148564	.317453	.171683
102	.033721	.076404	.038227	.035678	.082693	.040188	.115469	218648	.143632	.181788	.379763	.211458
103	.044562	.100915	.050531	.047620	.111101	.053575	.142965	265986	.178776	.224252	.465062	.261313
104	.058147	.136972	.065381	.063502	.156808	.070651	.166448	313481	.207218	.261918	.540855	.305469
105	.075476	.178990	.084782	.084158	.211238	.093406	.198604	378002	.246368	.309641	.665768	.356764
106	.103765	.235709	.117667	.120572	.315725	.132958	.240658	.402123	.312616	.367519	.667887	.448280
107	.133840	.307621	.151436	.156360	.374684	.175224	.307217	.609950	.376522	.477970	.999999	.552429
108	.190244	.411215	.218332	.236820	.586985	.263889	.384504	.660899	.493013	.595783	.999999	.715106
109	.261516	.532604	.304832	.334553	.865490	.370386	.508888	.781442	.684954	.790923	.999999	.979040

Table 14. Standard errors of the average remaining lifetime: Arizona, 1989–91

Exact age in years	Total Both sexes	Total Male	Total Female	White Both sexes	White Male	White Female	All other – Total Both sexes	All other – Total Male	All other – Total Female	All other – Black Both sexes	All other – Black Male	All other – Black Female
0	.049	.069	.065	.050	.071	.067	.187	.254	.268	.333	.451	.472
1	.046	.066	.062	.048	.068	.064	.183	.248	.262	.318	.429	.450
2	.046	.066	.062	.048	.068	.063	.182	.248	.261	.317	.427	.449
3	.046	.065	.061	.047	.068	.063	.182	.247	.261	.316	.426	.447
4	.046	.065	.061	.047	.067	.063	.182	.247	.261	.315	.425	.446
5	.046	.065	.061	.047	.067	.063	.182	.247	.261	.315	.424	.445
6	.046	.065	.061	.047	.067	.062	.181	.247	.260	.314	.423	.445
7	.046	.065	.061	.047	.067	.062	.181	.247	.260	.314	.423	.444
8	.045	.065	.061	.047	.067	.062	.181	.246	.260	.314	.422	.444
9	.045	.065	.061	.047	.067	.062	.181	.246	.260	.313	.422	.443
10	.045	.065	.060	.047	.067	.062	.181	.246	.260	.313	.422	.443
11	.045	.064	.060	.047	.067	.062	.181	.246	.260	.313	.421	.443
12	.045	.064	.060	.047	.067	.062	.181	.246	.260	.313	.421	.443
13	.045	.064	.060	.047	.067	.062	.181	.246	.260	.313	.420	.443
14	.045	.064	.060	.047	.066	.062	.181	.245	.259	.312	.420	.442
15	.045	.064	.060	.046	.066	.062	.181	.245	.259	.312	.419	.442
16	.045	.064	.060	.046	.066	.061	.180	.245	.259	.311	.418	.441
17	.045	.063	.060	.046	.066	.061	.180	.244	.259	.310	.416	.440
18	.044	.063	.060	.046	.065	.061	.180	.244	.259	.309	.415	.440
19	.044	.063	.059	.046	.065	.061	.179	.243	.258	.309	.414	.439
20	.044	.062	.059	.045	.064	.061	.179	.243	.258	.308	.412	.438
21	.044	.062	.059	.045	.064	.060	.179	.242	.258	.307	.411	.437
22	.044	.062	.059	.045	.064	.060	.178	.242	.257	.306	.410	.436
23	.043	.061	.059	.045	.063	.060	.178	.241	.257	.305	.409	.435
24	.043	.061	.058	.044	.063	.060	.178	.241	.257	.305	.408	.434
25	.043	.061	.058	.044	.063	.060	.178	.240	.256	.304	.407	.433
26	.043	.060	.058	.044	.062	.060	.177	.240	.256	.304	.407	.432
27	.043	.060	.058	.044	.062	.059	.177	.240	.256	.303	.406	.432
28	.043	.060	.058	.044	.062	.059	.177	.239	.256	.303	.406	.431
29	.043	.060	.058	.044	.062	.059	.177	.239	.255	.302	.405	.430
30	.042	.060	.058	.044	.061	.059	.177	.239	.255	.302	.405	.430
31	.042	.059	.057	.043	.061	.059	.176	.239	.255	.302	.404	.429
32	.042	.059	.057	.043	.061	.059	.176	.238	.255	.301	.404	.429
33	.042	.059	.057	.043	.061	.059	.176	.238	.255	.301	.404	.428
34	.042	.059	.057	.043	.060	.059	.176	.238	.254	.301	.403	.428
35	.042	.058	.057	.043	.060	.058	.176	.238	.254	.300	.403	.427
36	.042	.058	.057	.043	.060	.058	.176	.237	.254	.300	.402	.427
37	.041	.058	.057	.043	.060	.058	.175	.237	.254	.300	.402	.426
38	.041	.058	.057	.042	.059	.058	.175	.237	.254	.299	.402	.425
39	.041	.058	.056	.042	.059	.058	.175	.236	.253	.299	.401	.425
40	.041	.057	.056	.042	.059	.058	.175	.236	.253	.298	.401	.424
41	.041	.057	.056	.042	.059	.057	.174	.236	.253	.298	.400	.423
42	.041	.057	.056	.042	.058	.057	.174	.235	.252	.297	.399	.422
43	.041	.056	.056	.042	.058	.057	.174	.235	.252	.296	.398	.421
44	.040	.056	.055	.041	.058	.057	.173	.234	.252	.296	.397	.420
45	.040	.056	.055	.041	.057	.057	.173	.233	.251	.295	.396	.419
46	.040	.055	.055	.041	.057	.056	.173	.233	.251	.293	.395	.417
47	.040	.055	.055	.041	.057	.056	.172	.232	.250	.292	.393	.415
48	.039	.055	.054	.040	.056	.056	.171	.230	.249	.291	.391	.413
49	.039	.054	.054	.040	.056	.055	.171	.229	.248	.289	.389	.410
50	.039	.054	.053	.040	.055	.055	.170	.228	.248	.287	.387	.408
51	.038	.053	.053	.039	.055	.054	.169	.227	.247	.285	.384	.405
52	.038	.053	.053	.039	.054	.054	.169	.226	.246	.284	.382	.403
53	.038	.052	.052	.039	.053	.053	.168	.225	.245	.282	.380	.400
54	.037	.051	.052	.038	.053	.053	.167	.224	.244	.280	.378	.398
55	.037	.051	.051	.038	.052	.052	.166	.222	.243	.278	.375	.395
56	.036	.050	.050	.037	.051	.052	.166	.221	.242	.276	.373	.392
57	.036	.049	.050	.037	.051	.051	.165	.220	.241	.275	.371	.390
58	.035	.049	.049	.036	.050	.050	.164	.219	.241	.273	.369	.387
59	.035	.048	.049	.036	.049	.050	.163	.217	.240	.271	.367	.384

Table 14. Standard errors of the average remaining lifetime: Arizona, 1989–91—Con.

| Exact age in years | Total | | | White | | | All other | | | | | |
| | Both sexes | Male | Female | Both sexes | Male | Female | Total | | | Black | | |
							Both sexes	Male	Female	Both sexes	Male	Female
60	.034	.047	.048	.035	.048	.049	.163	.216	.239	.269	365	382
61	.034	.046	.047	.035	.048	.048	.162	.215	.238	.268	363	379
62	.034	.046	.047	.034	.047	.048	.161	.213	.237	.266	360	376
63	.033	.045	.046	.034	.046	.047	.161	.212	.237	.264	358	374
64	.033	.045	.046	.033	.046	.047	.160	.211	.236	.262	356	371
65	.032	.044	.045	.033	.045	.046	.159	.209	.235	.261	354	369
66	.032	.044	.045	.033	.045	.046	.159	.208	.235	.259	352	366
67	.032	.043	.045	.032	.044	.045	.159	.208	.234	.258	351	364
68	.032	.043	.044	.032	.044	.045	.158	.207	.234	.257	350	362
69	.032	.043	.044	.032	.044	.045	.158	.207	.234	.257	350	360
70	.031	.043	.044	.032	.044	.044	.158	.206	.234	.256	350	358
71	.031	.043	.043	.032	.043	.044	.158	.206	.233	.256	351	357
72	.031	.042	.043	.032	.043	.044	.158	.206	.233	.256	352	355
73	.031	.042	.043	.032	.043	.043	.157	.205	.232	.256	354	354
74	.031	.042	.043	.031	.043	.043	.157	.205	.232	.256	357	353
75	.031	.043	.042	.031	.043	.043	.158	.205	.232	.257	360	353
76	.031	.043	.042	.031	.044	.043	.158	.206	.233	.258	364	353
77	.031	.043	.042	.031	.044	.043	.159	.207	.234	.260	369	354
78	.031	.043	.042	.032	.044	.043	.160	.208	.235	.262	374	355
79	.031	.044	.042	.032	.045	.043	.162	.210	.237	.265	380	358
80	.031	.045	.042	.032	.045	.043	.164	.212	.240	.269	387	361
81	.032	.045	.042	.032	.046	.043	.166	.215	.243	.273	395	365
82	.032	.046	.043	.033	.047	.043	.169	.218	.246	.278	.405	370
83	.033	.047	.043	.033	.048	.044	.172	.222	.249	.284	.416	376
84	.033	.049	.043	.034	.050	.044	.175	.227	.253	.291	.430	383
85	.034	.050	.044	.034	.051	.045	.180	.233	.257	.299	.446	392
86	.035	.052	.045	.035	.053	.045	.185	.241	.263	.309	.467	.402
87	.036	.055	.046	.036	.056	.046	.192	.252	.270	.321	.494	.414
88	.037	.058	.047	.038	.059	.048	.200	.266	.279	.336	527	.428
89	.039	.061	.049	.039	.062	.049	.210	.285	.290	.353	569	.444
90	.041	.066	.051	.041	.067	.051	.223	.308	.303	.373	.622	.462
91	.043	.071	.053	.044	.072	.054	.236	.336	.318	.395	.684	.482
92	.046	.077	.056	.046	.078	.056	.251	.367	.333	.417	.752	505
93	.049	.084	.059	.049	.085	.060	.264	.396	.349	.438	805	528
94	.052	.091	.062	.052	.093	.063	.277	.421	.365	.456	814	553
95	.055	.098	.066	.056	.100	.067	.292	.450	.386	.472	.797	580
96	.061	.111	.073	.062	.113	.074	.315	.490	.415	.508	868	.622
97	.068	.126	.081	.069	.130	.082	.341	.540	.447	.549	957	.668
98	.077	.146	.091	.079	.151	.093	.370	.599	.483	.596	1 062	.719
99	.087	.170	.103	.090	.178	.106	.403	.656	.524	.648	1.166	.780
100	.101	.200	.119	.105	.212	.123	.442	.728	.572	.710	1 299	851
101	.118	.239	.139	.124	.257	.144	.489	.816	.633	.782	1.444	935
102	.141	.289	.164	.149	.318	.173	.545	.912	.705	.871	1.608	1 042
103	.169	.354	.196	.182	.399	.209	.607	1.017	.784	.966	1.792	1.155
104	.202	.434	.233	.223	.509	.254	.665	1.123	.859	1.056	1 965	1 264
105	.244	.525	.282	.275	.644	.312	.741	1.248	.961	1.169	2.179	1.403
106	.299	.637	.347	.348	.831	.393	.839	1.372	1.100	1.316	2 331	1.603
107	.360	.766	.417	.429	.999	.486	.964	1.672	1.244	1.522	2 853	1 823
108	.444	.913	.517	.551	1.340	.620	1.085	1.708	1.440	1.707	2 972	2 090
109	.499	1.001	.586	.641	1.626	.715	1.180	1.764	1.598	1.854	3.130	2 297

For a list of reports published by the National Center for
Health Statistics contact:

Data Dissemination Branch
National Center for Health Statistics
Centers for Disease Control and Prevention
6525 Belcrest Road, Room 1064
Hyattsville, MD 20782-2003
(301) 436-8500
Internet: www.cdc.gov/nchswww/

U.S. Decennial Life Tables, 1989–91

These 55 reports are published once each 10-year period by the National Center for Health Statistics.

VOLUME I

Number 1   *United States Life Tables.* This first report contains life tables by single years of age from birth to age 110 for the United States. Tables are included for the total population, the white population, the population other than white, and the black population. Within these large populations are tables showing the race-sex categories of male, female, and both sexes combined. Standard error tables for the probability of dying and of the average remaining lifetime are included.

Number 2   *Methodology of the National and State Life Tables.* This report describes in detail the methods of construction of the national and State life tables.

Number 3   *Some Trends and Comparisons of United States Life Table Data: 1900–1991.* This report deals with trends and interpretations related to life expectancy and survivorship.

Number 4   *United States Life Tables Eliminating Certain Causes of Death.* This report provides life tables analyzed by major groups of causes of death.

VOLUME II

Numbers 1 through 51   *Alaska through Wyoming, State Life Tables.* Each of these 51 reports contains life tables for a particular State and a table that ranks each State in the order of life expectancy. All States have tables for the total population and the white population by sex. In addition, 40 States have tables for the other than white population and 33 have tables for the black population. Standard error tables for the probability of dying and of the average remaining lifetime are included.

**DEPARTMENT OF
HEALTH & HUMAN SERVICES**

Centers for Disease Control and Prevention
National Center for Health Statistics
6525 Belcrest Road
Hyattsville, Maryland 20782-2003

OFFICIAL BUSINESS
PENALTY FOR PRIVATE USE, $300

DHHS Publication No. (PHS) 98-1151-3
8-0243 (4/98)